이스라엘 하마스 전쟁으로 본 중동 극단주의 흐름

The flow of **extremism in the Middle East** seen through **the Israel-Hamas war**

이스라엘 하마스 전쟁으로 본 중동 극단주의 흐름

2024년 7월 1일 초판 1쇄 발행

지은이 조다윗

도서출판 비전출판사
주소 서울특별시 서대문구 가재울로2안길 33 (03693)
전화 02-6414-7864
이메일 visionpd2@hanmail.net
홈페이지 www.wmuv.net
등록번호 제 312-2013-000011호

ISBN 979-11-87120-14-8 (93230)

© 조다윗 2024

The flow *of* extremism *in* the Middle East seen *through* the Israel-Hamas war

by David Cho

Copyright © 2024, by David Cho

이 책의 저작권은 저자와 도서출판 비전출판사가 소유합니다.
신저작권법에 의하여 한국 내에서 보호를 받는 저작물이므로
무단전재와 복제를 금합니다.

The flow *of* extremism *in* the Middle East seen *through* the Israel-Hamas war
Copyright 2024. Missionary David Cho and Vision Publishing House
all rights reserved.

이스라엘 하마스 전쟁으로 본
중동 극단주의 흐름

조다윗 선교사 지음

David Cho

The flow of **extremism in the Middle East**
seen through **the Israel-Hamas war**

차례

	머리말	11
	감사의 말	16
I	**이스라엘 하마스 전쟁으로 본 중동 이슬람 극단주의 동향 및 흐름 연구** - 아랍국가 내 팔레스타인 난민선교 가능성 및 전망	19
1	개요	21
2	하마스, 점조직 네트워크와 체제 시스템 이식의 집합체, 하이브리드 혼용 양상의 극단조직 경향과 흐름, 근원	27
3	알리야 운동 유대 시오니즘과 기독교, 팔레스타인 내 유대정착촌 구축 문제	41
4	역사적 관점에서 본 이스라엘, 팔레스타인 인접국가 -이집트, 요르단, 레바논 난민 수용 여부 및 난민선교 가능성	45
5	결론 및 전망	54

II 남겨진 민족 아랍의 기원과 연구과제, 시의적 아랍 상황 해석   59
- 아랍 부족주의 중심으로

1 **아랍의 기원에 관한 문제제기** - 아랍 부족주의의 근원을 생각해보며   61

2 **연구 제약을 넘어** - 아랍 유목문화 기록 부재와   63
헬라 지성에 수혈 받은 이슬람 지적 아카이브 활용

3 **성경에서 본 아랍의 기원**   65
- 이스마엘과 무함마드로 이어지는 아랍인 계보

4 **아랍의 기원 연구와 아랍학, 중동학, 이슬람학 개론 상**   67
연구 범주 재정립 - 북아프리카권, 중앙아시아권, 동남아시아권까지

5 **아랍 근원 부족주의와 무함마드,**   71
그리고 이스라엘 하마스 전쟁과 평화 해법

6 **아랍 이슬람 부족주의로 조명해 본 중동 소요 사태**   74

참고도서 및 서지정보   98

Contents

	Preface	105
	Thanks to	111
I	A Study on the trends and flows of Islamic extremism in the Middle East viewed from the Israel-Hamas war - Possibilities and prospects of Palestinian refugee missions in Arab countries	113
1	**Overview**	115
2	**Hamas, a discrete organization network and a complex of system transplantation. The trend of extreme organization with hybrid mixing aspects and its origin.**	123
3	Aliyah Movement, Jewish Zionism and Christianity, and the issue of establishing Jewish settlements in Palestine	142
4	**The possibility of refugee accommodation and refugee** - oriented missions in countries adjacent to Israel and Palestine (Egypt, Jordan, and Lebanon) from a historical perspective.	148
5	**Conclusion & Forecast**	159

II	**The origins and research tasks of the Arab - the remaining nation, Timely situational analysis** - Focusing on Arab tribalism	167
1	**Raising Questions about the Origins of Arabs** - Pondering the roots of Arab tribalism	169
2	**Beyond Research Constraints** - The absence of records of Arab nomadic culture and the Utilization of Islamic Intellectual Archives Injected with Hellenic Intellect	172
3	**The Origins of Arabs in the Bible** - The Arab lineage traces back to Ishmael and Muhammad	174
4	**Research on Arab origins and redefinition of research categories for introductory Arabic studies, Middle Eastern studies, and Islamic studies** - Including the North Africa region, Central Asia region, and Southeast Asia region	177
5	**Arab Root Tribalism, Muhammad, and Israel Hamas War and Peace Solutions**	182
6	**Examining the Arab Spring through the Lens of Arab Islamic Tribalism**	187
	Reference books and information	218

일러두기

이 글은 2024년 1월 경에 집필되었습니다.

『전방개척선교』 기고를 위해 칼럼형태의 글로 서두가 집필되기 시작하였음을 밝힙니다.

머리말

　세계 가운데 공간과 시간들이 뒤섞이고 있다. 고대와 중세 시간대의 정신성이 부활하여 초현대에 포개지는 양상이 부쩍 늘어나고, 지정학적 영역이 거의 달랐던 현상들이 기이하게 교차, 교직되어 이전의 관점으로만은 해석되기 어려운 사태들이 빠른 속도로 일어나 적층되며 새로운 시대성을 향해 나아가고 있다.

　고대 중세 관념의 이슬람은 이끼처럼 적층되어 중동 아랍권의 시대정신성을 여전히 그 시간대의 변주인 현상으로 발현, 반복 응용되곤 했다. 이슬람 극단주의 역시 무함마드 퍼스널리티와 칼리프 시대에서 모티브를 얻은 현상이었다. 그러나 무함마드나 하산 알 반나, 사이드 쿠틉의 제자라 할 만한 하마스가 전투자금이나 체제 유지 자금으로 가상화폐 비트코인을 활용하고 있는 것은 분명 고대나 중세에는 없었던 4차 산업 혁명기에 초현대 양상과 교직된 신종 현상이라 할 만하다.

　우크라이나와 전쟁을 치르고 있는 러시아에 ISIS 호라산

(ISIS-K)이 러시아 도시 한 복판에서 극장 테러를 감행하였다. 그리고 나토(NATO)의 결집 앞에 북·중·러 간의 구소련 친연성을 자극해 서방과 대결을 벌이고 있는 러시아의 양태가 신냉전 시대를 부활시키는 것인가 하는 학자들의 오피니언도 있다. 이 가운데 이슬람 극단주의자들이 신냉전 대결의 축인 러시아로 진입해 폭탄테러를 가하고, 이를 곧 ISIS 소행임을 인정하면서도 배후에 우크라이나가 도사리고 있다는 푸틴의 주장을, 현대 신냉전의 틀이나 고대 이슬람 종교정신성의 극단적 적층 현상인 이슬람극단주의에 대한 분석틀로만 해석될 수 있을까?

더불어 우크라이나와 러시아 전쟁 간 인공지능(AI)이 사람을 살상하는 결정권한을 집행한 일이 이미 일어난 것은 또 얼마나 빠른 시의적, 시대적 변화의 전조인가? 이렇게 인공지능 프로그램이 사람을 살상하는 일, 즉 죽음과 생명을 가를 일을 결정하는 현상이 이미 일어나고 있는 시대적으로 빠른 변화를, 어떻게 하면 성경적으로 진단하고 선지자처럼 미리 해석해낼 수 있을까?

이번 책은 세계의 시간과 공간이 뒤섞이는 이러한 현상이 더욱 빈번해지고 있는 경향 가운데 학제적 연구와 전통적 학문 연구가 따라잡기 어려울 정도로 빠르게 일어나는 신종현상과 시의적 정보가 넘쳐나는 시대 속, 작은 연구 결과물이다. 전통적 학문은 귀납적 연구에 따라 인간의 지적 오류를 검증하는 틀을 지녔다. 더군다나 학제적 연구는 두 가지 이상의 여러 학문적 관점을 종합해 시공간이 뒤섞이고 있는 현상에 대응코자 한다.

그러나 이러한 전통학문을 통한 지성 형성의 지난한 과정은, 인간의 지적 주장 갱신, 생성에 오류를 검증하고자 논문 등의 형태를 통해 패러다임 형성 기반, 일반화할 수 있는 객관적 근거 타당성, 교차검증 등에 학문적 정제를 수반하여 시간적 소요가 꽤 많이 필요하다. 이미 초현대 현상은 빠르게 일어나고 적층되며 시의적 IT정보가 넘쳐나는데 반해, 전통적 학문의 약점은 그 철저한 검증절차에 비해 속도가 너무 더디다는데 있다.

이스라엘 하마스 사태는 전통적 학문 논문 정보보다, IT정보, SNS, 실시간 동영상 등으로 세계에 알려지게 되었다. 학자들도 그 세계에 들어가 연구하고 논문적 정제를 거치기보다 현상이 너무 빠르게 번져가고 세계에 막대한 영향을 미치기 때문에 이러한 IT 정보에 근거하여 사태, 현상을 해석하여 오피니언으로 즉시 의견을 발표하는 일이 잦아졌다.

다만 이러한 IT 정보는 신속한 정보 파악이 가능한 반면 전통적 학문의 검증 없이는 인간의 지적 정보 인지에 편향적 오류 등을 걸러 내기 어렵다는 치명적 약점이 존재한다. 따라서 이제는 전통적 학문과 IT 정보 사이에 서서 신속하고 비교적 적확한 지적 해석을 해내는 눈이 세계에 필요하다.

결정적으로, 모든 고대부터 초현대까지 인류 역사는 결국 성경의 진리에 수렴되어 해석되어야만 한다. 이슬람을 발현시킨 아랍이 성경에 나오는 이스마엘의 후손이며, 성경은 이미 그의 삶과 세계관을 해석해 놓았다.

또한 인공지능이니, 비트코인이니 하는 것들이 4차 산업혁명에 해당되는 신종 테크놀로지 현상이기는 하나, 고대 바벨탑 이야기에는 당시 신종 테크놀로지인 아스팔트 류의 역청을 개발한 인간의 속성을, 성경은 이미 해석한 바 있다.

따라서 이러한 세계에 시공간이 섞이고 시대적 변화가 빠른 지금, 학제적 연구와 IT 정보류의 홍수 속에서 성경적 관점으로 해석해내는 진리의 사람들이 더욱 긴요하다. 이 졸저가 작은 모티브나 질료가 되었으면 좋겠다.

2024년 4월 초

우크라이나 러시아 전쟁 인공지능의 살상 소식을 접하며,
이스라엘 헤즈볼라 이란 선전 포고의 암운 속에,
흔들리지 않는 진리를 푯대로 붙잡는 마음 가운데

조다윗 선교사

감사의 말

책이 나오기까지 많은 영감에 자양분이 되어 준 믿음의 선진들과 더불어, 교정과 편집 작업을 도와준 유경은 간사, 박혜지 간사, 고상한 북디자인을 해 준 권혁기 간사, 영문 번역을 맡아준 박시원 간사, 반하은 간사, 김희명 간사, 비전 선교 공동체와 함께하는 350여명의 선교 사역자들 모두 감사하다.

말씀과 함께 살기 위해 공동체의 삶을 마다않고 더불어 함께 하는 아내와 은빛, 시후, 안녕이를 비롯한 가족들은 내 보석들이다. 우리가 아니더라도 누군가를 통해 주님이 어두운 시대를 밝힐 말씀의 횃불을 드실 것이나 말씀이 우리와 함께 하심에, 그래서 감사하다.

The flow of **extremism in the Middle East** seen through **the Israel-Hamas war**

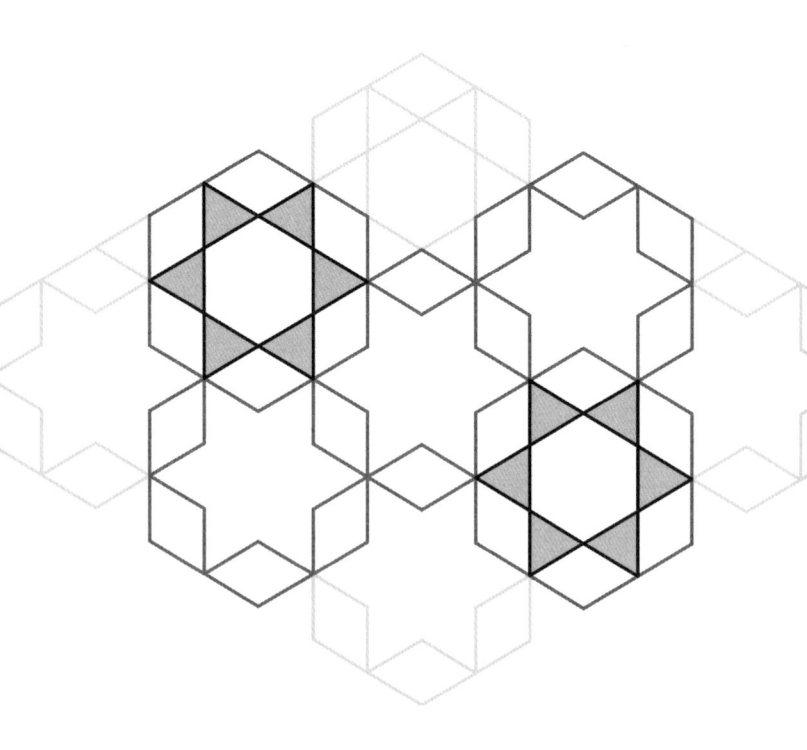

I

이스라엘 하마스 전쟁으로 본
중동 이슬람 극단주의 동향 및 흐름 연구

- 아랍국가 내 팔레스타인 난민선교 가능성 및 전망

1 개요

2000년 전후 냉전시대를 마감하면서 9.11 사태[1]를 통해 세계는 이슬람 테러리즘과 서구의 대립 양상으로 지구적 갈등의 축이 전환된 측면이 있었다. 9.11 사태를 추동시킨 오사마 빈 라덴(Osamabin Laden)과 알카에다(Al-Qaeda)[2]는 갑자기 등장한 이슬람 극단주의 점조직 네트워크 운동이 아니라, 이미 오래전부터 이집트 무슬림 형제단(Muslim Brothers)[3] 2대 지도자 '사이드 쿠틉(Sayyid Qutb)[4]'의 대서구 무장투쟁 폭력노선 이슬람 극단주의 사상에 영향을 받은 운동가들이었

---

1 2001년 9월 11일 발생한 미국 뉴욕의 110층 세계무역센터(WTC) 쌍둥이 빌딩과 워싱턴의 국방부 건물에 대한 항공기 동시 다발 자살테러 사건. 이 사건으로 약 3천여명에 가까운 사망자가 희생되었다.

2 미국에서 발생한 9.11테러 배후세력으로 지목된 오사마 빈 라덴이 조직한 수니파 극단주의 테러조직.

3 약 500만~1000만 명에 추정되는 회원 수를 가진 세계 최대·최고(最高)의 이슬람주의 단체로 이집트의 이슬람학자이자 사회운동가인 하산 알-반나(Hasan al-banna)가 1928년 '진정한 이슬람 가치의 구현과 확산'을 목표로 수에즈의 이스마일리야에서 설립한 이슬람 근본주의 조직이다.

4 이슬람 극단주의 이론과 행동철학을 다듬고 체계화하여 이슬람 극단주의 운동의 새로운 이정표를 제시한 '이슬람 이데올로기화'와 '이슬람 혁명'이론의 주창자이다. 오늘날 이집트를 비롯한 무슬림 세계 전역에서 일어나고 있는 이슬람 극단주의 운동에 있어 가장 영향력 있는 인물 중 하나로 평가 받는다.

다. 미국은 아프가니스탄 탈레반 전쟁으로 말미암아 알카에다 등 이슬람 테러리즘 점조직 네트워크(network) 궤멸을 목표로 삼았다. 그러나 이로 인해 세계 국경을 넘어 산개된 이슬람 극단주의 점조직 네트워크의 궤멸이 달성되었다기보다도, 이라크 전쟁 이후에는 전란의 혼란을 틈 타 오히려 ISIS[5]가 등장하여, 이슬람 극단주의 체제 이식 시도가 활보해, 시리아, 이라크 등지에서 칼리프 시대 이슬람국가를 표방하는 극단주의 체제(system) 이식기를 낳았다. 이는 9.11 직후 알카에다로 대변되는 이슬람 극단주의 점조직 네트워크 운동기에 비해 더욱 악성적인 ISIS로 부각된 이슬람 극단주의 체제 이식 시도였다.

주지하다시피 2023년 10월 팔레스타인 하마스(Hamas)[6]

---

[5] 급진 수니파 무장단체인 이라크-레반트 이슬람국가(ISIL로 일컬어지기도 함). 2003년 알카에다의 이라크 하부조직으로 출발한 단체로, 급격히 세력을 확장해 2014년 이슬람국가(IS)로 개명하며 아부 바크르 알바그다디를 칼리프로 추대하고 이라크와 시리아를 중심으로 세력을 확장했다. 2017년 7월과 10월에 걸쳐 각각 이라크 모술과 수도인 시리아 락까를 잃으면서 와해됐다. 이후 2019년 3월 시리아민주군(SDF)에 의해 마지막 근거지였던 바구즈까지 상실했다.

[6] 이스라엘에 대한 테러를 주도하고 있는 팔레스타인의 대표적인 무장단체로, 파타와 함께 팔레스타인 양대 정파를 구성하고 있다. 1987년 인티파다 당시 아메드 야신에 의해 설립됐으며, 2006년 팔레스타인 총선에서 승리한 후 2007년 가자지구에서 파타를 몰아내고 독자적으로 가자지구를 통치하고 있다.

테러조직 무장정파로 인해 유대 민간인 등을 납치 살해, 전쟁 포로로 억류하는 일련의 잔인한 사태가 촉발, 하마스 이스라엘 간 전쟁이 발생하였다. 이미 베냐민 네타냐후(Benjamin Netanyahu) 총리 수반 내각과 이스라엘 정부는 시오니즘(Zionism)에 입각한 근본주의 경향을 강하게 띠는 상태였고[7], 유대 불법정착촌[8] 등의 문제가 서안지구에서 팔레스타인과 유대인 간에 폭력 갈등을 유발하고 있는 즈음이기도 했다.[9]

이러한 배경 하 국가전을 대리할 만한 전쟁 사태를 유발한 하마스는 과연 어떤 조직인가? 그들은 알카에다와 같은

---

7 2022년 11월 네타냐후 총리가 재집권에 성공하며, 극우 세력 결집 성공을 기반으로 집권한 이번 정부는 이스라엘 역사상 가장 극우 성향을 띤다는 평가를 받고 있으며, 강경한 팔레타인 정책과 사법개혁으로 인해 이스라엘 정세가 불안정해지던 상황이었다.
이지은, 「베냐민 네타냐후 총리 재집권 이후 이스라엘의 정세 변화와 시사점」, 『KIEP 세계경제 포커스』, Vol.6 No 6, KIEP 대외경제정책연구원, 2023.

8 팔레스타인 자치지역인 가자지구와 요르단강 서안지구에 있는 유대인 거주 지역을 일컫는다. 국제사회는 이스라엘이 1967년 제3차 중동전쟁을 통해 점령한 서안지구 등에 유대인 정착촌을 건설하는 것을 불법으로 규정하고 중단을 요구하고 있다. (국제사법재판소 및 유엔 안전보장이사회)

9 "서안지구 내 정착촌 건설이 긴장과 폭력을 야기해 항구적 평화 정착을 방해한다"며 안토니우 구테흐스(UN 사무총장)는 이스라엘 내 정착촌과 관련된 모든 활동을 즉각 중단할 것을 촉구했다.
AL JAZEERA AND NEWS AGENCIES, "Israeli settlers set up new illegal outpost on Palestinian land", ALJAZEERA, 2023.06.22.

점조직이 유발하는 비대칭전쟁[10]에 테러조직인가? 그들은 이스라엘 뿐 아니라 카타르, 터키에도 지부를 두고 있다는 점에서 국경을 넘어서는 점조직 네트워크이기도 하다. 또한 그들은 국가와 같은 정권장악에 거버넌스 체계(governance), 시스템인가? 물론 그들은 팔레스타인에서 2006년 이후 선거를 통해 정권을 장악한 정파이기도 하다.[11] 그들은 2000년대 이후 이슬람 극단주의 경향에 부각되어 순차적으로 나타난 점조직 네트워크(network) 양상의 알카에다 형태를 띤 테러리즘과, 거버넌스 체계를 구축한 극단주의 체제(system)로서의 ISIS 양상의 면모를 동시에 혼재한 하이브리드 형태에 점조직이자 시스템 곧 거버넌스 체계이다.

이것은 근래 일어난 이슬람 테러리즘 동향에 따라 알카에다나 ISIS의 영향만 받았다기보다도, 하마스가 이집트 무슬

---

10 상대적으로 군사력, 전략 또는 전술이 크게 다른 교전단체 간의 전쟁 유형이다. 적군이 국가 정규 군대가 아닌 분쟁을 의미하며, 반군, 저항운동, 유격전, 대 분란전, 테러리즘, 대테러 활동 등을 포함한다.

11 2006년 1월 25일, 팔레스타인 자치정부의 입법회 총선에서 하마스가 44.45%, 전체 의석 132석 중 74석을 차지하며 승리했다.
Ali Abunimah, "Hamas Election Victory: A Vote for Clarity", The Electronic Intifada, 2006.01.26.

림 형제단의 팔레스타인 지부격으로 출범한 연유를 살펴야 한다.[12] 때문에 무슬림 형제단 출현 근원에 내재되어 있던 정파 조직이면서도, 그 후 무장투쟁 테러노선을 좀 더 가미했던 조직 전신에서 그 모티브와 근원을 찾아야할 듯하다. 따라서 무슬림 형제단의 500여 지부를 창설 가능케 한 '하산 알 반나(Hassan Al Banna)'[13]라는 설립자의 교사 교원공무원으로서 배경과 그에 따른 이슬람 근본주의 운동의 정파 정치체계(system) 접근과, 2대 지도자인 사이드 쿠틉이 무장투쟁 노선을 무슬림 형제단에 가미한 배경을 설명해 그의 사상을 통해 무장투쟁노선의 테러리즘이 점조직 네트워크(network)로 활성화된 영향력을 기술코자 한다. 더불어 지면이 허락한다면 이스라엘과 북쪽에서 대치하고 있는 전선을 살피며, 이란 호메이니(Ayatollah Ruhollah Khomeini)가 이란 신정 근본주의 이슬람 정권을 수립[14]하면서 이름과 강령을 하사 출범된 시아

---

12 2017년도 42조 헌장을 수정내용을 발표하기 전까지 하마스는 무슬림형제단의 지부임을 공식적으로 인정했다. 박현도(서강대학교 유로메나연구소 교수), 2023.
https://youtu.be/FW0XOfgoiYk?si=s29eMR9k0qNj2vil

13 손주영, 황병하 외, 『1400년 이슬람 문명의 길을 걷다』, 프라하, 2012, p736.

14 "호메이니가 제시한 국가체제는 '이슬람법학자통치제제'로 신정과 공화정의 하이브리드 형태이다." 인남식(국립외교원교수 및 중동연구부장), 2022.
https://youtu.be/0dv_vZR1oLQ?si=m4flMeZUZfWhdmiz

파 극단주의 정파 헤즈볼라에 시스템과 점조직이 혼재된 경향, 부각 양상을 짚어보고자 한다.

또한 유대 불법정착촌 문제는 이스라엘의 우경화, 근본주의적 시오니즘을 통해 종교적으로 알리야 운동(Aliyah)[15] 등을 펼치며 유입된 디아스포라 유대인들의 귀환과 해외 개종 유대인의 유입 문제와 관련이 있다. 일부 기독교에서 이러한 운동을 지지 지원하는 흐름이 있는데 이러한 영향이 어떻게 불법정착촌 문제를 가중시켰는지도 종교적 사상만이 아니라, 국제 지역학적 관점으로도 진술하고자 한다. 그리고 이 글 막바지에는 중동에 막대한 충격과 영향력으로 발휘되고 있는 근본주의 극단주의 노선 하에 현장 최신 이슈를 짚으면서도, 전란 가운데 발생한 난민에 요르단, 이집트, 레바논 인근 국가의 수용 가능성을 역사적 배경 하에 엿보고 팔레스타인 난민사역에 접근성을 타진해보고자 한다.

---

15 전세계에 흩어진 유대인 디아스포라들이 유대인의 땅인 이스라엘 본토로 귀환하는 운동. 1950년 이스라엘 의회에서 통과된 귀국법은 모든 디아스포라 유대인과 그들의 자녀 및 손주들에게 유대인 정체성과의 연결을 바탕으로 이스라엘로 이주하고 이스라엘 시민권을 취득할 수 있는 권리를 부여한다.

2 하마스, 점조직 네트워크와 체제 시스템 이식의 집합체, 하이브리드 혼용 양상의 극단조직 경향과 흐름, 근원

군사강대국인 이스라엘을 상대하여 국가를 대리해 전쟁을 벌이고 있는 하마스는 점조직 네트워크와 시스템의 양쪽 면모를 동시에 지니고 있다는 점에서 2000년대 이후 등장한 이슬람 근본주의 조직 알카에다에 점조직 네트워크 운동, ISIS 체제 이식의 시도를 혼종한 하이브리드된 양상을 가졌다. 알카에다는 시민사회와 전선의 구분이 모호한 가운데 [16] 비대칭전쟁을 유발한다는 점에서, 강대국 미국을 괴롭혔고, ISIS는 중동일대에 칼리프체제 이식을 자체 현실화함으로써 한동안 중동을 혼란으로 몰아가 국제적 난제로 작동되었다.[17] 극단주의 네트워크와 시스템이 2000년대와 2010년대

---

[16] 빈 라덴은 수단에서 비지니스와 테러가 융합된 대규모 조직체를 설립했다. 알카에다 대원이 빈 라덴의 투자 회사 대표직을 가지고 서유럽에서 극동까지 다니며 비지니스 기업과 비정부 단체 등을 조직했다. 동시에 그 사무소들을 테러활동을 위한 재정과 기타 여러 필요를 지원하는데 이용했다.
9/11위원회, 「미국에 대한 테러 공격에 관한 국가 위원회의 최종 보고서(The 9/11 Commission Report)」, 2004, p.57.

[17] 에이미 추아, 김승진 역, 『정치적 부족주의』, 부키, 2020, p.137-143.

순차적 파고를 통해 부각되어, 어떤 세계적 문제와 폐해를 나타내는지를 역사적 시대적으로 보였다.

하마스가 앞 선 두 조직에 비해 비교적 작은 조직이긴 해도, 두 조직의 네트워크와 시스템 양상의 효과적으로 발휘하는 혼종 조직으로 기능하고 유사한 이슬람 극단주의 조직이 중동에 하이브리드된 형태로 등장한다면 알카에다나 ISIS에 비해 결코 세계와 중동가운데 폐해가 작지 않을 수 있어 선교 상황에 입각해서도 예의주시해야 할 것이다.

어쨌든 이러한 하마스의 점조직 네트워크이자, 거버넌스 정부 체제, 체계의 시스템인 양상은 기존 이슬람 극단주의 사상가나 운동가 하산 알 반나, 꾸틉, 오사마 빈 라덴 등의 면모에 영향을 받거나, 근본주의, 극단주의 조직 무슬림 형제단, 알카에다, ISIS에 시대적 반향에 따라 상호 영향을 받아 구축되었다 할 수 있겠다. 따라서 하마스라는 무슬림 형제단의 팔레스타인 지부로서 출발해 현재는 팔레스타인의 정부 체제로서 존재하며, 터키·카타르[18] 등지에 점 조직을 가지고 있는

---

[18] "하마스의 정치국 위원은 자금 모집과 외교정책을 결정한다. 이들은 현재 카타르에 안가를 제공받고 있다." 성일광(고려대학교 중동이슬람센터 교수), 2023. https://youtu.be/syyO6bQNfF0?si=ArG0yqZSArZp7Jju

양면적 형태를 지닌 이 조직에 두 면모의 모티브나, 깊이 영향을 준 극단주의 사상가, 운동가, 조직 등을 살펴봄으로써 어떻게 하마스가 체제이면서도 점조직 네트워크를 갖추었는지, 또한 이를 통해 부각되는 최근 동향의 이슬람 극단주의 면모에 근원 소스를 파헤쳐보고자 한다.

1) 무슬림 형제단 창설자 하산 알 반나
- 500여 점조직 운동지부 설정과 대 이스라엘 지하드19로 인한 정치 조직화

하마스는 이집트에서 유학했던 야신(Sheikh Ahmed Yassin)[20]이라는 인물을 통해 세워져, 먼저 무슬림 형제단 팔레스타인 지부로 시작되었다. 따라서 이집트 무슬림 형제단의 성립과정과 사상적 배후에 막강한 영향을 받았다 할 수

---

19 지하드의 의무수행을 마음에 의한 것, 펜에 의한 것, 지배에 의한 것, 칼에 의한 것의 4가지로 구분하고 있지만 지하드가 폭력, 선동의 이미지를 갖게 된 것은 급진적 무장조직이 자신들의 테러활동을 위해 대중 선동하기 위해서 사용하였고, 서구 역시 이슬람을 자신들의 문명사회에 대한 도전으로 정치 도구화하여 사용한 결과이다.

20 팔레스타인 가자지구 난민 출신으로 이집트에서 수학했으며, 인티파다에 참여했고 이후 이스라엘을 공격하기 위한 하마스를 창설. 무장투쟁을 시작했으며 종교서적, 설교, 연설 등으로 대중조직화사업을 펼쳤다.

있다. 무슬림 형제단의 창시자인 하산 알 반나는 교사 출신으로서 정부체계에 교원 공무원에 일원이었다. 당시 오스만 칼리프 제국이 서구에 패퇴하여 이집트에서도 오스만 지배 예속의 영향력이 감퇴된 것은, 한편 곧 오스만 칼리프 제국 자체가 이슬람의 보루라 여겼던 무슬림들에게 역사적으로 꽤 충격적인 일이었다.[21] 이러한 무슬림들의 충격 속에 하산 알 반나는 이슬람 정신의 새로운 구심점이 필요하다고 느껴, 1928년 22세 나이에 무슬림 형제단을 창시하고 이는 종교 운동, 정치 운동으로 사회 전반에 스며들어 곧 500여 지부가 점조직이자 운동형태로 무슬림 사회 각지에 생성되는 파급효과를 낳았다. 하산 알 반나는 이집트와 무슬림 사회에 이슬람 칼리프 체제[22] 복원을 목표로 무슬림 형제단을 창설했는데 이는 점조직 운동이 칼리프 체제 구현을 목표로 추구한다는 점에서 곧 정파, 정치화를 지향하게 되었다. 또한 1933년 팔레스타인 땅에 이스라엘인이 이주해오는 일이 늘어나자 하산 알 반나는 이에 대항하는 지하드를 펼쳐야할 필요성을 호소했고,

---

[21] 손주영, 황병하 외(2012), 앞의 책, p.739.

[22] 아랍어로는 본래 '칼리파트 라술 알라(Khalifat rasul Allah)'로 그 사전적 의미는 '신의 사도의 대리인'이다. 칼리프는 예언자 무함마드의 뒤를 이어 이슬람 교리의 순수성과 간결성을 유지하고, 종교를 수호하며, 동시에 이슬람 공동체를 통치하는 모든 일을 관장하는 이슬람 제국의 최고 통치자를 가리킨다.

이 때문에 1939년에는 무슬림 형제단이 실제로 정치조직화되어 점진적으로 재편되어갔다.[23]

2) 무슬림 형제단 2대 지도자 사이드 쿠틉
– 현대 이슬람 극단주의 사상가, 무장과격투쟁노선, 테러리즘 도입 단초를 열다

설립자 하산 알 반나를 통해 반 이스라엘 저항운동이 정치조직화 된 후 꾸틉이 무슬림 형제단의 2대 지도자가 되어 조직을 점점 더 과격노선으로 이끌어갔다.

이는 꾸틉 개인의 서구에 대한 소외 경험에서 비롯되었다. 이집트에서 태어난 사이드 쿠틉은 미국으로 유학을 떠난다. 똑똑하고 예리한 지성을 지닌 사이드 쿠틉은 미국 유학 시절, 개인주의적인 서구인들의 행태에 심각한 소외감과 외로움을 느끼고, 자존심에 상처를 받았다. 이윽고 꾸틉은 서구사회의 약점을 일제히 경험적 토대로 분석하고,[24] 세계 시스템에 있어 서구 기독 세력의 타락이 악의 근원이라 규정하

---

23 손주영, 황병하 외(2012), 앞의 책, p.745-747.
24 손주영, 황병하 외(2012), 앞의 책, p.749-752.

기에 이른다.[25] 거룩한 이슬람 문명권에서 온 중동인 꾸틉의 눈으로 보면, 거룩한 알라의 명령을 지키고자 율법의 일점일획까지 지키려 노력하는 거룩한 무슬림들이 타락한 서구 문명에 지배받거나 지배 주도권을 내어주는 것은 역사적 정당성이 없어보였다.

다시 말해, 꾸틉이 경험한 서구는 물질과 섹스, 쾌락과 향락으로 타락한 곳이었고, 거룩한 이슬람 중동 문명을 지배하고 무슬림을 모욕하는 이러한 서구는 정당성이 없는 주도 권력일 뿐이었다. 세계 1, 2차 대전 이후 대 중동 문명에 대해 완전히 주도 권력을 확보한 서구 문명은 거룩한 율법을 지키는 중동 무슬림들을 하인과 정원사, 집사 등으로 부려왔다. 그러나 무슬림에게 보여준 서구인들의 삶의 태도는 유흥과 마약 등에 찌들고 섹스와 향락에 빠진, 더러운 물질로 인격을 마음대로 부리는 타락한 양상일 뿐이었다.

꾸틉은 결국 이슬람의 지하드 개념을 확장하여 단순히

---

[25] '서구 기독교 세계가 주는 현재의 힘든 환경이 주는 압박과 지하드에 대한 사악한 오리엔탈리스트들의 공격이 있다.' '전능하신 알라는 오로지 진실을 말씀하셨다. 역사를 왜곡하는 기독교 세계의 사기꾼들은 모두 거짓말쟁이들이다'
사이드 꾸틉, 서정민 역, 『진리를 향한 이정표(이슬람 원리주의 혁명의 실천적 지침서)』, 평사리, 2011, p.184, 337.

이슬람 통치로써의 지하드가 아니라 투쟁으로써의 지하드 개념을 적극 활용하면서, 이슬람을 오염시키고 있는 악의 근원인 타락한 서구 문명 세계의 축출과 저항을 천명했다.[26] 이로써 꾸틉은 이슬람 지역 내부에 국한되었던 지하드 개념을 국제화하며 투쟁 개념은 곧 테러와 무력 사용에 사상적 단초를 제공했다.[27] 꾸틉에 강력한 영향을 받아 세워진 이집트의 무슬림 형제단은 현재 무력 강경 투쟁 노선을 온건 노선으로 선회하긴 했지만 현존하는 대부분의 이슬람 극단주의 테러 단체의 실제적인 정신적 모태가 되어왔다.

 이러한 사상은 곧 오사마 빈 라덴 등에 수혈되어 알카에다, 점조직 네트워크를 통한 9.11사태를 발생시켜 국제적 대서구 투쟁노선, 글로벌 지하드 점조직 운동기를 추동하는데 막대한 영향력을 끼쳤다.

---

26 사이드 꾸틉(2011), 앞의 책, p.148-153.

27 극단주의 이슬람 성직자 오마르 압델 라흐만은 1990년 이집트에서 미국으로 건너가, 사이드 쿠틉의 '진리를 향한 이정표' 내용으로 설교했다. 그는 미국을 세계 무슬림의 억압하는 나라로 규정하며 '신의 대적'에 맞서 싸우는 것이 의무라고 주장했다.
9/11위원회(2004), 앞의 보고서, p.72.

3) 오사마 빈 라덴과 알카에다
   – 이슬람 극단주의 운동가,
      로컬 지하드에서 글로벌 지하드로의
      실천적 전환, 알카에다를 통한
      글로벌 점조직 네트워크 운동기 작동

9.11사태를 일으킨 오사마 빈 라덴은 이슬람 지역에 머물렀던 지하드의 방향을 글로벌 지하드로 선회시킨 운동가라는 점에서 현대 이슬람 극단주의 운동의 상징적 인물이라는 것은 주지의 사실이다.[28] 꾸틉의 사상을 수혈 받은 빈 라덴은 이슬람을 타락시키고 오염시킨 체제가 미국을 비롯한 서구 체제임을 분명히 하며, 로컬 지하드 운동으로는 극단주의가 신봉하는 무함마드 시절의 이슬람 원형을 찾기 어렵다고 판단한다. 종교적이고 지역적인 지하드가 아니라, 이슬람 체제를 오염시키고 지배한 서구의 체제를 이슬람에서 영구 축출

---

28 빈 라덴이 1998년 2월에 전쟁을 선포할 때, 그는 휘하에 10여 년 동안 모병하고 훈련해왔던 실질적이고 세계적인 군사 조직을 보유하고 있었다. 또 다른 극단주의자들이 지역정권이나 이스라엘을 목표로 하는 것이 충분하지 않다고 여기며 미국 공격에 집중할 것을 촉구했다. 동시에 자신이 미래의 새로운 운동력임을 주장했다. 9/11위원회(2004), 앞의 보고서, p.54-55.

하기 위해 지하디스트[29]들 표현에 의하면 '악의 머리인 미국의 본토를 공격해야 한다'는 선언과 실천을 감행한 것이다.[30]

    따라서 꾸틉의 이슬람 극단주의, 지하드 사상체계를 본격적으로 글로벌 운동기나 점조직 네트워크 작동기로 이끈 인물이 오사마 빈라덴이라고 보아야 한다. 그는 이슬람 지역에 머물렀던 로컬 지하드 흐름을 9.11 사태로 단번에 글로벌 지하드 운동으로 바꾼 인물이다. 종교 이맘들에게 지하드라는 개념은 무슬림들이 알라의 뜻에 복종해야 할 종교적 계율이었고, 근대 극단적 지하디스트들에게도 지하드는 이슬람 지역 내에서 혹은 그 경계 어간에서 이루어지는 지역적 무력 투쟁이었다. 그러나 오사마 빈라덴은 지하디스트들의 극단주의 운동력을 단순히 이슬람 지역 경계 어간에서가 아닌 글로벌 지하드로 전환한 국제적 운동력을 추동한 인물로서,

---

29 다음과 같은 경전의 구절이 지하디스트들에게 투쟁의 동기가 된다. "침략하는 자들에 대항하며 투쟁하는 것이 너희에게 허락되나니 모든 잘못은 침략자들에게 있노라. 알라는 전지전능하사 너희에게 승리를 주시니라." (쿠란 22:39)
30 에이미 추아(2020), 앞의 책, p.145.

글로벌 지하드의 국제 지도력, 상징적 아이콘이 되었다.[31] 또한 국경을 넘어선 알카에다 점조직 연동으로 그들이 주적으로 설정한 미국을 비롯한 서구에 대항, 국가 대 국가의 형태가 아닌 비대칭전쟁을 통해 최소한의 전력으로, 강대국을 상대하는 면모를 보였다.

4) 체제 이식으로의 ISIS
– 이슬람 칼리프 제국의 복원, 극단주의 체제 이식 시도

이슬람 칼리프 체제의 복원을 천명하는 ISIS에는 영웅적 인물이나 그 이름이 부각되지 않는다. 왜냐하면, 행동가나 운동가의 활동을 넘어 ISIS는 체제 이식을 꿈꾸고 있기 때문이다. 자연스럽게 인물보다는 이슬람 국가라는 체제에 더욱 역점을 두고 있다. 무함마드와 그 후계 체제였던 칼리프 체제의 이슬람 확장기 역사만이 이슬람 극단주의자가 인정하는 오

---

31 오사마 빈라덴이 알카에다 및 해외 추종자들에게 이슬람국가 형성에 앞서 미국과 서구 집중 공격을 촉구하는 전략과 지시내용을 담은 문서가 공개되었다. NBC News, 2015.05.22., "Bin Laden Documents Revealed | NBC Nightly News"

염되지 않은 원형의 이슬람이다.[32] 칼리프 체제가 종식되고, 혈통적 세습으로 통치되던 이슬람 왕조체제는 이미 원형의 이슬람이 아니라는 것이다.

따라서 ISIS를 비롯한 지하디스트들은 이슬람 체제의 원형(Prototype)인 이슬람 칼리프 체제의 복구와 복원만이 세상을 향한 답이 될 수 있다고 믿는다. 지하디스트들에 따르면 무함마드와 칼리프들을 통해 알라가 나타낸 이슬람 통치 원형으로서의 제정일치 이슬람 제국은 혈통적 세습체계가 아니었다. 이슬람 체계의 원형은 영적 지도력에 따른 영도체계로 권력이 이양되던 칼리프 체계였다. 지하디스트들은 코란과 순나[33] 즉, 알라의 샤리아 법은 오직 이 원형의 칼리프 체제만을 인정한다고 믿는다. 심지어 그들은 서구 체제는 물론 혈

---

32 초창기 무슬림들은 한 가지 샘물을 마셨기에 역사상의 다른 세대와는 구별되는 특별한 세대로 남을 수 있었다. 하지만 시간이 지나면서 이 샘물에 다른 근원과 가르침이 섞이기 시작했다. 후대의 무슬림들은 그리스 철학과 논리학, 고대 페르시아의 설화와 사상, 유대교의 경전과 전통, 기독교 신학, 그리고 이와 더불어 다른 여러 종교와 문명의 찌꺼기들까지 받아들여 순수한 이슬람을 오염시켰다.
사이드 꾸틉(2011), 앞의 책, p68-69.

33 아랍어로 '관행(慣行)'을 뜻한다. 무함마드에 의해 이슬람교가 창시된 후로는 순나의 의미에도 변화가 생겨, 무함마드의 언행 등, 이슬람교도가 모범으로 삼아야 할 것을 가리키게 되었다.

통적 세습 왕조의 이슬람 국가들도 변형된 체제라 여겨 배격한다. 따라서 알라의 샤리아 법이 명령한 이 칼리프 체제를 복원하는 것이야말로 알라의 법에 복종하지 않는 세계의 타락과 오염을 바로잡을 유일한 방법이라는 것이다.[34]

그래서 극단주의자들은 글로벌 지하드로 세계에 이슬람 극단주의 운동을 추동하면서 단순히 지하드 운동가들의 점조직적인 네트워크를 구축하는 것이 목적이 아니라, 이러한 네트워크를 기반으로 칼리프 체제를 복원하는 꿈을 실현시키길 원한다. 지하디스트들은 칼리프 체계야말로 알라의 법이 명령한 유일한 이 땅의 체제라 생각하며, 그들에게 이는 서구 자유주의, 민족주의, 사회주의, 왕조체제 등에 오염된 중동 체계를 일시에 제거, 변혁할 이상향적인 투쟁 목표가 된다.[35]

---

34 "초창기 무슬림들이 가르침을 받았던 그 순수한 근원, 즉 다른 것과 섞이거나 오염되지 않은 가장 순수한 근원으로 돌아가야 한다. 그리고 그 순수한 근원으로부터 우리의 삶, 정부 시스템의 근간, 정치, 경제 등 모든 분야의 기준을 정립하고 해답을 찾아내야 한다."
사이드 꾸틉(2011), 앞의 책. p75.
35 "결과적으로 초창기 무슬림들과 같은 역량을 갖춘 사람들의 무리가 현 시대에 나타나지 않고 있다. 때문에 이슬람 운동을 추진해나가기 위해, 그리고 이를 위한 훈련과 교육을 시작하기 위해 현재 우리의 주변에 팽배해 있는 자힐리야의 영향과 잔재로부터 우리 자신을 분리해 내는 것이 절대적으로 필요하다." 꾸틉은 현재 이슬람권 국가들도 자힐리야로 간주해 극단적 이슬람주의 투쟁의 대상으로 삼았다.

또한, 무함마드와 칼리프가 보여주었듯이 전쟁을 통해 칼리프 체제가 확장되었던바, 7세기경에 무함마드와 칼리프가 활용한 전술 전략이 고스란히 정당화된다. 그것은 '헤지라(Hegira)[36]'라고 하는 무함마드가 메카에서 이주한 사건 이래, 진격전은 물론 칼리프 시대까지 이슬람 확장 수단으로 사용되었던 전시 상황에 일어난 포획, 거짓과 선동 전술, 이주를 통한 전시 유불리 상황 역전, 심지어 노예제도와 여성의 납치·유린까지도 초기 이슬람체제가 보여준 그대로 정당성을 부여한다. 따라서 칼리프 체제가 복원될 때까지 이슬람 극단주의 전사들은 알라의 뜻이 완전히 이루어지는 성스런 지하드의 개념으로 이러한 투쟁을 두려움 없이 정당화하고 당연시한다.[37] 즉, 이들은 이것을 종교적 신념으로 정당화하고 있기에 매우 위험한 가치와 체계를 이 땅에 이식하려는 것이라 할 수 있다.

---

36 622년 9월 25일, 예언자 무함마드가 쿠라이쉬족의 박해를 피해 메카에서 야스리브(Yathrib, 후의 메디나)로 이주했다. 이 사건으로 이슬람은 종교적, 사회적 질서로 자리 잡게 되었고, 이는 이슬람력의 시작점이 되었다.
브리태니커 편찬위원회, 『브리태니커 필수 교양사전 이슬람』, 아고라, 2017, p43.
37 "이러한 투쟁은 일시적인 것이 아니다. 알라의 권위가 전 지구에 확립되어야만 하고……"
사이드 꾸틉(2011), 앞의 책, p152.

이에 따라 칼리프 국가 건설이라는 지하디스트들에게 있어 이상향적 목표를 제시한 알 바그다디(Abu Bakr al-Baghdadi)[38]가 ISIS를 천명하고 단체를 정비해 더 자극적이고 선동적인 방법으로 잔인한 테러와 투쟁을 이어가자 실제적 투쟁에 목마른 많은 지하디스트들이 ISIS로 몰려갔다. 그들은 칼리프 정부체계를 조각하고, 경제체제 구축을 위해 칼리프 시대 단위의 화폐를 발행하는 등 국가와 체제 이식의 의도를 뚜렷이 보여주었다.[39] 이로써 이 땅에 칼리프국가 복원과 칼리프체제 이식을 꿈꾸고 있는 많은 지하디스트들의 동경과 지지, 그리고 합류를 이끌어내기에 이르렀다.[40] 민병대 8천 명 수준의 ISIS지하드 전사들이 감히 이슬람 칼리프 제국을 복원하겠다고 공언하는 신념의 기저에는 죽음도 불사하겠다는 종교적인 신조가 내포되어 있고 이것을 집단체제화

---

38 이라크 바그다드 성직자 출신으로 뛰어난 조직력과 전술로 독립적인 세력을 결성하여 이라크와 시리아 일대에 수니파 칼리프국가를 세우고 스스로를 '새로운 칼리프'로 칭했다.

39 "사담후세인 정권 하에 수십 년간 실질적으로 이라크 정부체제를 운영해왔던 관료들이 대거 ISIS에 합류했다", 인남식, 위즈덤칼리지, 2023.

40 '보이지 않는 지도자'로 은둔하며 활동하다 모술의 그랜드 모스크 금요기도시간에 '새로운 칼리프 이브라힘'이라고 등장하여 추종자들을 모으기도 했다.
Martin Chulov, The Guardian, 2014.07.06, "Abu Bakr al-Baghdadi emerges from shadows to rally Islamist followers"

한다는 점에서 그 심각성이 있다고 할 수 있었겠다.

3 알리야 운동 유대 시오니즘과 기독교, 팔레스타인 내 유대정착촌 구축 문제

이번 전쟁에 원인이 된 요소 가운데 하나가 유대인들의 팔레스타인 지구 내 불법정착촌 구축이었다. 이스라엘과 팔레스타인, 국제사회가 협정[41]으로 맺은 서안지구 및 가자지구와 이스라엘 경계는 서로의 존립을 인정하는 최소한의 선이었다. 유대인들도 기존 유럽 등지에서 인종청소의 위협을 경험한 민족이나, 다시 이스라엘로 돌아와 나라를 세우면서 팔레스타인 아랍인들을 아예 제거해야 한다면 모든 민족을 구원(마24:14)[42] 하길 원하시는 말씀과 신약 기조 상 옳은 일인지 기독인들이 신중히 생각해봐야 할 문제다. 이스라엘 정부

---

41 1967년 아랍-이스라엘 3차 전쟁 이후 현재 국경선이 정해졌으며, 이후 미국의 중재로 1978년에 이집트와 이스라엘이 캠프데이비드협정을, 1993년에는 이스라엘과 팔레스타인(PLO)이 오슬로협정을 맺었다.

42 이 천국 복음이 모든 민족에게 증언되기 위하여 온 세상에 전파되리니 그제야 끝이 오리라.

가 우경화되면서, 해외에서 유입된 유대개종자들을 중심으로 팔레스타인 경내로 불법정착촌을 구축하여, 총포 등으로 무장한 경비 병력을 보내 팔레스타인과의 마찰에서 보호와 자구책을 가지려했다. 하마스와 이스라엘 전쟁이 개진되면서 서안지구에도 불안한 정세가 이어져 불법정착촌에 정착한 유대인들이 불안을 느껴, 팔레스타인들에게 총격을 가하고, 이스라엘에 저항하는 서안지구 팔레스타인의 시위도 계속되고 있다.[43]

특이한 점은 불법정착촌에 정착한 상당수에 유대인들이 해외에서 율법과 할례를 지키겠다는 전제로 유대인으로 개종한 해외 이민자들이라는 점이다. 이는 알리야 운동과 깊은 연관이 있는데 이를 위해 네팔, 중국, 우크라이나, 카자흐스탄, 수단 등지에서 이방인들까지 유대인으로 개종시키는 각

---

[43] 시오니즘에 입각한 유대인 불법 정착촌 확장과 유대인 유입으로 국제사회의 우려가 커지고 있다. 이스라엘은 2023년 상반기에만 서안지구에 5,700채의 신규 주택 건설 계획을 허가했다. 이미 동 기간에 13,000여개의 주택이 완공되었으며 이는 2022년의 3배에 달하는 규모다. 이에 6월에 정착민 4명이 팔레스타인의 공격으로 사망하며 정착민에 대한 폭력사태가 이어졌다.
BBC NEWS, "Israel backs new Jewish settlement homes", 2013.08.11.
Yolande Knell, "West Bank: US 'troubled' by Israeli settlement expansion plans", BBC News, 2023.06.27.

지역 캠프를 열어 이방인을 유대인화하고, 이들을 이스라엘 가나안 땅으로 고토 복귀시키는 직간접적 지원 운동이 벌어지고 있다. 이스라엘 내부는 이미 인구 밀집도가 높아 귀환한 이들이 팔레스타인 경내 이스라엘 불법정착촌에 뿌리 내리도록 장려되고 있는 실정이다.[44]

알리야 운동은 유대인들이 바벨론 유수기를 경험하며 구약의 성전 근처에서 멀어지는 것이 저주이며, 성전 근처 고토로 복귀하여 예루살렘 성전으로 올라가는 것이 복이라 생각해서 구약 배경 바벨론 포로기에 흩어진 유대인들의 상황 가운데 체계화된 사상이다. 다만 이 운동을 선의로 구약적 배경에 친연성을 느끼는 기독인들이나 교회가 지원하는 경향이 있는데, 이 알리야 운동 저변에 이스라엘 고토와 유형의 성전을 신성시하는 생각은, 신약기조 상 예수 그리스도가 유형의 건물이나 지역이 아닌 믿는 우리 마음 가운데 성전이 되셨다는 기독교의 교리와는 차이가 있다. 또한 이방인이 다 돌아

---

[44] 일부 알리야 운동에 참여한 유대인들 중에는 개신교였던 사람들이 이스라엘로의 이주 지원을 받는 사례도 있다. 개도국의 경제적 여건을 회피하려는 수단으로 알리야 운동을 이용하기 위해 개종하는 경우로 보인다.
https://m.blog.naver.com/khchojh/222902469245

온 뒤에 유대인들이 예수그리스도께 돌아오게 된다는 로마서의 바울의 견해[45]는 복음이 모든 민족가운데 전해지는 가운데 유대민족을 향해 예수를 메시아로 영접하게 하는 구원의 계획이 남아있음을 의미한다. 다만 알리야 운동은 이방인들을 율법과 할례를 지켜 유대인이 되게 하는 개종 운동인 바, 바울이 이방인들 선교에 있어 이방인들이 먼저 율법과 할례를 지켜 유대인이 되어야만 구원 받는다는 다른 복음에 대해 경계했던 기독 교리[46]를 되새겨볼 필요가 있다. 이방인인 네팔, 수단 등지의 민족들이 먼저 유대인이 되는 입문식, 율법도 지키고 할례를 받아 유대인으로 개종하게 되면 유대인들의 종교교리를 받아들이게 된다. 게다가 나사렛 예수를 구원자로 여기지 않아 이스라엘에 나라의 독립과 정치적 해방을 이루어줄 시오니즘에 입각한 메시아를 기다리는 유대인들의 안티기독교의 종교적 신념까지 학습될 수 있다.

물론 기독교인들이 막대한 물량과 직간접 지원으로 이방

---

45 형제들아 너희가 스스로 지혜 있다 하면서 이 신비를 너희가 모르기를 내가 원하지 아니하노니 이 신비는 이방인의 충만한 수가 들어오기까지 이스라엘의 더러는 우둔하게 된 것이라. 그리하여 온 이스라엘이 구원을 받으리라(로마서 11:25-26)

46 그리스도께서 우리를 자유롭게 하려고 자유를 주셨으니 그러므로 굳건하게 서서 다시는 종의 멍에를 메지 말라. 보라 나 바울은 너희에게 말하노니 너희가 만일 할례를 받으면 그리스도께서 너희에게 아무 유익이 없으리라(갈라디아서 5:1-2)

인까지 유대인들로 개종시켜 유대 고토로 귀환시키는 운동을 도와준데 대해 유대인들이 그 선의를 고마워할 수 있고 기독인들에 대해 우호적인 마음을 갖게 될 수 있다. 그럼에도 과연 이방인들까지 기독인이 아니라 유대인들로 개종 시키고자 하는 알리야 운동에 기독교인들의 열심이 막대하게 투여되는 것에 제고가 필요해 보인다.

4 역사적 관점에서 본 이스라엘, 팔레스타인 인접국가–이집트, 요르단, 레바논 난민 수용 여부 및 난민선교 가능성

1) 이집트

이집트는 전화에 휩쓸린 팔레스타인 가자지구가 이스라엘의 지구 봉쇄, 하마스 고립을 위한 살라미 전술[47], 지하화된 하마스 궤멸을 위한 상시 공습, 폐허화로 인해 사방이 고

---

[47] 하나의 과제를 여러 단계별로 세분화해 하나씩 해결해 나가는 협상전술의 한 방법으로, 얇게 썰어 먹는 이탈리아 소시지 '살라미(salami)'에서 따온 말

립된 가운데 유일하게 팔레스타인 가자지구와 국경을 맞댄 국가이다. 또한 국제사회의 구호활동, 물자공급을 위해 국경 출입을 허용하고 있기도 하다. 그렇다면 약 600만이 넘게 발생되고 있는 팔레스타인 난민[48]을 아랍형제국가의 호의로서, 또는 국제아랍사회의 수뇌, 머리를 자처하는 이집트는 팔레스타인 난민을 수용할 것인가? 안타깝게도 전망은 결코 낙관적이지 않다.

이집트의 현 엘시시(Abdel Fattah Al Sisi) 정권은 군부쿠데타를 통해 무르시(Mohamed Morsy) 전 대통령을 권좌에서 축출한 집단이다.[49] 무르시는 중요소요사태의 여파로 정국의 혼란가운데 민의를 통해 집권한 대통령으로 국제사회에 표면적으로 알려져 있으나 이면적으로는 무르시가 무슬림 형제단 출신이며 수뇌였다.[50] 따라서 무르시를 축출한 군부출신 엘시시 현직 대통령과 그 정권은 무슬림 형제단이 이집트

---

48 유엔 팔레스타인 난민 구호 사업 기구(United Nations Relief and Works Agency for Palestine Refugees in the Near East, UNRWA) 발표(2023)

49 하현정, 「이집트, '빵, 자유, 정의'라는 오래된 문제로의 회귀」, 『아랍의 봄 그 후 10년의 흐름』, 서울대학교출판문화원, 2022, p.42-44.

50 무슬림형제단의 일원일 당시 무소속 정당으로 국회에 선출되었으나 2005년 이집트 정부의 탄압으로 의석을 잃고, 무슬림 형제단의 지도부로 임명되었다.

의 막강한 막전막후의 영향력으로 작동하면서 또 직접 정파나 배후로서 그 영향력 안에 있는 인사를 통해 다시 정권을 손에 넣을 수도 있다는 불안감이나 정적의식을 가지고 있다.

따라서 하마스가 무슬림 형제단의 팔레스타인 지부 전신이며, 아랍 이슬람을 결집시킬 이슈, 예루살렘, 이스라엘 등의 문제를 안고 이집트로 허용된 난민 가운데 하마스 조직원들이 틈타 들어올 것을 어느 역대 정부나 정권에 비해 경계할 수밖에 없다. 다시 말해, 하마스 조직이 실체를 일반 팔레스타인 시민사회에 은닉·은폐하는데 능수능란하기 때문에, 이집트가 난민을 허용할 경우 자칫 난민사회에 은닉된 하마스 수뇌나 조직원들이 이집트로 흘러들어오는 것을 극히 경계하여 난민 수용을 허용할 가능성이 거의 없다고 여겨진다.[51] 이전에 이번 하마스 전쟁과 무관한 팔레스타인인들이 이집트에 난민으로 정착하는 것에 대해 국제사회로부터 다분히

---

[51] "미국의 경제적 지원을 받고 있는 이집트를 위시한 아랍권의 군부국가들은 하마스와 같은 단체가 자국 내 이슬람 혁명 등의 문제를 일으키리라 보고 꺼린다." 성일광, 2023.
https://youtu.be/syyO6bQNfF0?si=ArG0yqZSArZp7Jju

요식행위를 치루고 있다는 평가가 주를 이른 바,[52] 이번에 발생한 난민을 적극적으로 이집트 정부가 수용할 가능성은 극히 적어보인다.

2) 요르단

요르단은 아직 전화에 본격적으로 휩쓸리지 않은 팔레스타인 서안지구와 국경을 맞댄 나라다. 역사적으로 이스라엘 정부와 팔레스타인 자치정부 수립 직전에는, 근원방의 팔레스타인 아랍족들이 요르단 토후국에 속하였다는 의식도 존재했다.[53] 따라서 요르단은 팔레스타인 난민이 발생할 시 난민 수용에 가장 우선적인 고려대상 국가가 될 수 있다. 그럼에도 불구하고 요르단은 역사적으로 서안지구에 통치권을 가지고 있는 파타당(Fatah Party)[54]에 한 전신 흐름이었던 PLO(

---

52 가자지구와 외부(이스라엘 제외)가 연결된 유일한 라파 검문소 개방에 대한 권한이 이집트에 있다.
BBC News 코리아, "'가자 지구의 생명줄'이 된 이집트 국경 라파 검문소란?", 2023.11.02.

53 브리태니커 편찬위원회(2017), 앞의 책, p.198, 207.

54 1957년 1월 1일 야세르 아라파트(Yasser Arafat)가 중심이 되어 조직한 팔레스타인해방기구(PLO)의 중요 정당

팔레스타인 해방기구, Palestine Liberation Organization)⁵⁵ 아라파트(Yasser Arafat)[56] 수반과 반목하여 내전에 준하는 전투를 치른 적이 있다.[57] 아라파트와 PLO가 이스라엘과 평화협정에 나서는 등 무장투쟁노선에서 돌아서서 소강국면에 온건파로 변모된 측면이 있지만, 원래는 대 이스라엘 투쟁에서 무력노선을 가지고 있었으며 이스라엘 간 대립에서 열세에 놓여 투쟁기반을 요르단으로 이동시킨 적이 있었다.

그러나 대 이스라엘 간 아라파트 무장투쟁전선은 아이러니하게 자신들에게 망명, 투장기반을 허용한 요르단 정부와 반목, 긴장을 유발하는 상황을 초래했고, 곧 이는 아랍 형제 나라 요르단과 총부리를 겨누고 싸우는 사태를 가져온다. 결국 요르단 정부는 이내 아라파트와 PLO를 추출하여 자국

---

[55] 팔레스타인 독립국가 건설을 목표로 1964년 결성된 비밀 저항조직으로, 1993년 9월 이스라엘과 가자·예리코시의 자치에 관한 오슬로 중동평화협정에 참여하였고 현재 팔레스타인 자치정부(PNA)로 변신해 합법적으로 존속하고 있다.

[56] 팔레스타인 해방기구(PLO)의 초대 수반이자 팔레스타인 자치정부(PNA) 의장을 역임했던 인물로, 40여 년간 팔레스타인 독립투쟁을 이끌었다. 이스라엘에 대한 저항의 상징이자 팔레스타인의 국가적 영웅으로, 생전 독립투사와 테러리스트라는 상반된 평가를 동시에 받았으며 1994년에는 이스라엘의 이즈하크 라빈, 시몬 페레스와 함께 노벨 평화상을 수상하였다.

[57] 검은 9월(Black September)로 알려진 기간 동안 아라파트는 요르단 후세인 국왕의 "파시스트 정부"를 전복하라고 명령했다.
BBC News, "1970: Civil war breaks out in Jordan"

내에서 내쫓았다.[58]

이와 같은 역사적 경험으로 비추어 볼 때, 요르단 정부는 팔레스타인인들을 형제라 칭하나 여전히 무력투쟁노선을 고수하는 하마스가 난민과 함께 섞여 들어와 팔레스타인에서 기반을 잃어버리고 점조직이나 망명형태로 요르단에 정착하는 것을 극도로 경계할 수밖에 없겠다. 따라서 요르단이 가자기구에서 발생한 난민들을 적극적으로 수용할 가능성 역시 많지 않겠다.

3) 레바논

레바논 역시 앞서 말한 요르단의 경우보다 심각하게 요르단에서 쫓겨난 아라파트가 레바논 남부를 주요거점으로 대이스라엘 무력투쟁을 전개하는 것을 허용하다 아예 내전에

---

58 1971년 초에 아라파트와 PLO는 요르단에서 추방되었다.
Pierre Tristam, "Black September: The Jordanian-PLO Civil War of 1970", ThoughtCo., 2019.07.03.

휩싸인 역사적 상흔이 존재한다.[59] 레바논은 특이하게도 공화정 형태이나 종교인 비율로 마론파(Maronites) 기독교, 수니파(Sunni) 이슬람, 시아파(Shi'a) 이슬람 종파 등이 분권적으로 권력을 나누는 특이한 국가형태를 가지고 있다. 이렇게 종파별로 권력을 나누는 형태의 레바논 정부의 특성 가운데 아라파트가 남부 거점으로 대 이스라엘만이 아닌 레바논 내부에서 일으킨 마찰과 충돌은 종파별로 자경단 형태를 띠는 레바논 종파별 무장세력 할거를 출현시키고 곧 이는 오랜 내전을 유발했다.[60]

아라파트가 대 이스라엘 투쟁에 망명 거점으로 삼은 레바논 남부는 가난하며, 정부 권력 분점으로부터 비교적 소외된 시아파가 주류를 이루고 있었는데, 이러한 낙후와 혼란기를 틈타 시아파를 주축으로 외부 외세의 원조를 통해 흥기한

---

59 1970년대 레바논으로 넘어온 PLO 게릴라와 팔레스타인 민병대가 레바논 기독교 정파 간의 충돌로 1975년부터 15년간 내전이 이어졌다. 이 내전으로 10만 명이 넘는 사망자가 나왔다.
이경수, 「레바논, 모자이크 사회와 통합을 위한 국민의 외침」, 『아랍의 봄 그 후 10년의 흐름』, 서울대학교출판문화원, 2022, p.156.

60 "종파주의에 기반을 둔 레바논 사회는 자연스럽게 후견주의(clientelism)를 낳았다. 이러한 후견주의는 국민이 국가가 아닌 종파의 지도자들에게 충성을 맹세하게 해 각 종파 지도자가 자신을 맹목적으로 따르는 민중을 쉽게 선동할 수 있게 한다."
이경수, 앞의 책, p157-160.

세력이 바로 시아파 무장정파 헤즈볼라[61]이다. 이란의 호메이니는 1979년 이란에 이슬람 시아파 신정근본주의 정권을 수립한 후,[62] 1982년 레바논 내 시아파를 지원하여 이스라엘 축출을 강령으로 한 헤즈볼라 창설을 추동하여 '신의 당, 이슬람 지하드'라는 뜻의 헤즈볼라 명칭을 하사하였다.[63] 이는 곧 이슬람 극단주의 경향으로 이 글에서 짚고 있는 체제이자 점조직 연동의 형태와 유사하다.

이러한 헤즈볼라를 통해 이스라엘 북부 전선확대가 국제사회에 노심초사되고 있는 실정이다. 헤즈볼라는 10여 년간 시리아 내전에서 점조직 형태의 형제 시아파 무장단체를

---

61 1983년 창설된 레바논의 이슬람 시아파 무장세력이자 정치 정당으로, 1979년 이란 시아파 혁명과 1982년 이스라엘 침공에 이어 레바논 시아파 성직자 집단이 이스라엘을 레바논에서 몰아내고 그곳에 이슬람 국가를 세우자는 목표 아래 헤즈볼라를 조직했다.
브리태니커 편찬위원회, 앞의 책, p245.

62 "종신직 최고 종교 지도자가 헌법수호위원회를 통해 대통령, 내각, 국회에 이슬람법에 따라 개입한다.", 인남식, 2022.
https://youtu.be/0dv_vZR1oLQ?si=m4flMeZUZfWhdmiz

63 "이란은 이슬람 부흥운동이라는 자신들의 운동 유형을 이웃 이슬람 국가에 전하려고 노력하기도 했다.",
브리태니커 편찬위원회(2017), 앞의 책, p233.

지원하느라 소모전을 치러왔기에[64] 이스라엘과 먼저 전면전을 개진할 가능성은 적어 보이나, 산발적 미사일 공방전, 이스라엘이 대 하마스 전 승기를 자신하게 되면, 이스라엘이 레바논과 헤즈볼라를 상대로 전면전을 개진할 가능성도 아예 배제할 수만은 없다.[65]

이와 같이 불안한 산발적 전선은 레바논의 난민 수용 가능성을 어둡게 한다. 또한 전술한대로 과거 아라파트와 PLO가 온건노선 전에 무장투쟁노선으로서 레바논을 대 이스라엘 투쟁에 거점으로 삼았다가 레바논에 혼란과 내전을 유발한 역사적 상흔에 측면을 고려하면 역시 레바논이 팔레스타인 난민을 하마스와 구분 없이 수용할 가능성이 많지 않다 전망할 수 있겠다.

---

64 헤즈볼라는 바샤르 알 아사드 시리아 대통령의 확고한 동맹으로, 2011년 시리아 내전이 격화됐을 때 아사드 대통령을 위해 무장 대원 수천 명을 파견했다.
BBC News 코리아, "레바논 무장단체 헤즈볼라는 누구인가?", 2023.10.18..

65 지난 1월 2일, 8일 이스라엘이 공습으로 헤즈볼라 고위 간부 살레 알 아루리와 최고 사령관 위삼 알 타윌을 살해했다. 또한 요아브 갈란트(이스라엘 국방장관)의 최근 인터뷰 중 "가자에서 일어나고 있는 일이 베이루트에 '복사 붙여넣기'가 될 수"있다고 강조했다.
Dario Sabaghi, "Are Hezbollah and Israel edging closer to war?", THE NEW ARAB, 2024.01.15.
Laila Bassam and Maya Gebeily, "Israeli strike kills a Hezbollah commander in Lebanon", REUTERS, 2024.01.09.

5 결론 및 전망

하마스는 팔레스타인 무슬림형제단 지부로 출발하여, 이집트 무슬림형제단 하산 알 반나의 칼리프 체제 확립을 목표로 하는 체제 이식의 함의를 수혈 받아 정파, 정권 체제 이식의 형태를 지녔다. 동시에 하산 알 반나가 국가를 넘어 500여 지부 점조직을 무슬림 세계에 작동 시켰던 운동 네트워크의 면모도 닮았다. 하마스는 팔레스타인 내에만 존재하는 것이 아니라 카타르, 터키 등지에도 지부, 점조직을 두고 있다. 무슬림 형제단 2대 지도자 꾸틉의 영향을 받은 현대 여러 이슬람 극단주의 운동 조직처럼, 무력 투쟁 노선으로서의 테러, 시민사회와 전선을 넘나드는 비대칭 전쟁을 유발하여, 강대국 이스라엘과 맞서려 하고 있으나, 오사마 빈라덴의 알카에다처럼 전세계에 폭넓은 점조직을 갖추었다고 보기는 어렵다. 또한 ISIS처럼 체제 이식의 면모를 보이기는 하나, ISIS가 테러, 납치, 공개 처형 등 무함마드 초기 칼리프 역사, 프로토 타입 형태의 악성적 체제 이식을 시도하여 이슬람 극단주의에 대해 전세계의 환멸을 사고, 8천명 수준의 지하디스트를 한 지역에 체제로 묶어 놓는 바람에 강대국과 비대칭 점조직형태의 국경없는 전선이 아닌 체제 대 체제로 대립함으로써 지리멸렬하였던 것과는 미묘하게 다른 형태를 지닌다.

하마스는 정파 정권 체제의 이식이긴 하나, 자체 부패 가운데에서도 국제구호품 매개 전달 등을 맡아 민의에 기반한 동조를 얻어야 했던, 선거에 기반한 정권인 만큼, ISIS에 체제 이식의 모티브 면모를 가졌으나, 아랍지역에 일부 민의에 동조, 기반하고, 호소하는 측면을 지녔다. 헤즈볼라 무장 정파도 역시 국회의원을 배출[66]할 만큼 지역의 민심에 호소, 소구, 동조해야하는 측면을 지녔다는 점에서 ISIS처럼 악성적 체계의 휘발적 붕괴보다 그 자생력이 체제로서 길 가능성이 높다. 후티 반군, 헤즈볼라, 하마스 등 체제와 연동된 점조직 형태의 원리, 극단주의 운동이 여러 대륙에서 지역 로컬에 호소, 소구되고 일부 민의를 얻어 자생하고 있다.[67] 그 가운데 점조

---

[66] 1992년 8명의 국회의원 배출 후 2005년부터 내각에 주요 정당으로 참여했다. 2022년 총선에서는 13석을 유지했다.
Kali Robinson, Council on Foreign Relations, "What is Hezbollah? What to know about its origins, structure and history", PBS NEWS HOUR, 2023.10.16.

[67] 후티 반군 지도자들은 예멘의 부족체계에 능통하며 살레 전 대통령의 네트워크를 활용해 많은 부족 동맹을 확보했다.
ACLED, "Increasing tribal resistance to Houthi rule", reliefweb, 2019.03.07.

직 네트워크 운동성을 가지면서 이슬람 극단주의 체제 및 네트워크에 직간접 아랍세계 연동성을 갖는다면, 알카에다와 ISIS 기존에 부각되었던 이슬람 원리주의, 극단주의 조직이 혼재된 양상에 강약점을 지닌 채, 극단주의에 새로운 경향을 지닌 파고의 시대를 만들 가능성이 있다.

이러한 혼재된 이슬람 정파, 극단주의 조직이 ISIS보다 길게 자리매김하고, 알카에다의 세계 점조직 운동성에는 미치지 못하나, 점조직을 기반한 채 각자 로컬을 운영하는 체제를 만들면서도, 하마스, 헤즈볼라, 후티 반군처럼 적대 이스라엘 등에 공통 이슈로 서로 느슨한 연대를 지닌다면 중동 세계에 만만치 않은 파장과 혼란, 갈등을 유발할 수 있겠다. 다시 말해 암세포처럼 ISIS 악성 체제 이식을 위해 주변을 휘발, 황폐화시킨 전례[68]와 똑같지 않게, 단기간 내에 붕괴되기 쉽지 않은 로컬 체제들로 계속 자리 잡을 수 있어 보인다.

몸 글에서 전술한대로 안타깝게도 팔레스타인 난민 사

---

68 IS 점령지역 하에 구금되었던 민간인들과 8천명이 넘는 실종자들에 대한 조처가 시급하며, IS 소속 전사들이 통제되지 않는 채 시리아에 혼란을 야기할 수 있으며, 이라크에도 심각한 영향을 미치며 위협이 되고 있다.
Simon Tisdall, "The collapse of Isis will inflame the regional power struggle", The Guardian, 2019.02.17.

역에 대한 접근에 전망이 밝지만은 않다. 그럼에도 앞으로 중동 분쟁의 유동성 증가를 전망할 때, 기존 시리아 난민 등 요르단 등지에 난민 사역에 길이 열려 있을 시점까지는, 충분하게 사역 접근을 해야 한다. 이러한 극단주의 혼재 양상으로 중동에 언제, 어느 지역의 불안정성이 증가될 지 예측하기 어렵다. 난민은 불안정성으로 본향을 떠난 자들이고, 이슬람 전체주의적 사회, 본향에서 떨어져 나와 개인의 선택이 가능한 곳으로 이동할 수 있는 사람들이기에 현재 중동권 난민 사역은 열려있는 지역으로 더욱 사역을 집중해야한다. 이슬람 극단 정파, 점조직 혼재 양상으로 아랍 내 불안정성이 증가되며, 예측 불허한 중동 갈등이 각 로컬마다 돌발적 양상으로 나타날 수 있는 바, 난민 사역에 기회와 기간이 한정적 일 수 있다는 자세로 사역이 열린 곳에 최선의 기독 역량을 투여해야 할 것이다.

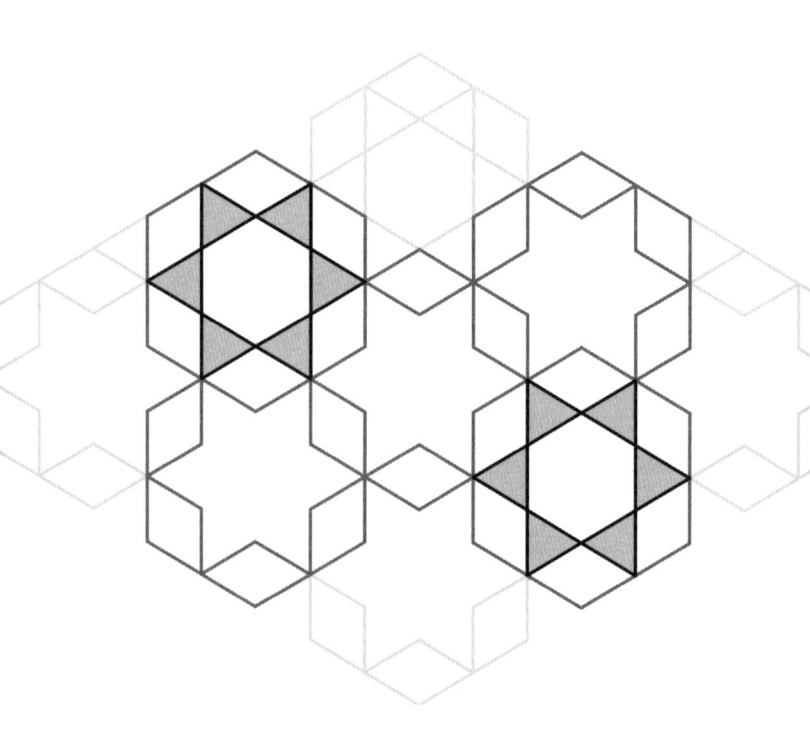

2

남겨진 민족
아랍의 기원과 연구과제,
시의적 아랍 상황 해석
- 아랍 부족주의 중심으로

1 아랍의 기원에 관한 문제제기
– 아랍 부족주의의 근원을 생각해보며

중동학, 이슬람학, 아랍학에는 이상하리만치 아랍에 관한 기원이 간과되거나 7세기 이전 역사가 미진하게 다루어진다. 이슬람을 열어 중동·북아프리카·중앙아시아·동남아시아 등지에 거대한 영향을 미친 아랍족은 희한하게도 내외부의 역사가들로부터 아랍 민족 기원과 근원에 대해 간과된 채로, 7세기 이후에 이슬람 종교의 체계화로부터 역사서술이 본격화되는 경우가 대부분의 아랍을 다루는 역사서술 방식이다. 아랍민족은 7세기 이후에 갑자기 등장하여 이슬람 종교를 체계화하여 따르고 전파한 민족인가? 아랍 민족은 7세기 이전부터 존재해왔다. 그런데도 왜 아랍을 기원으로 한 이슬람, 중동 연구 역사에서 아랍민족의 근원이 간과된 측면이 강할까?

아랍사를 다루는 관점에서 있어 무함마드를 비롯한 이

븐 할둔(Ibn Khaldun)[1] 등 아랍 내부자로서 아랍 역사에 막대한 영향을 끼치거나 역사관점을 정립한 권위자들이 있다. 일단 이슬람을 창시한 무함마드는 아랍 역사에 있어 막강한 영향을 끼친 것이 주지의 사실이다. 그러나 그는 이슬람 이전의 아랍을 자힐리야(Jahiliya)[2]라는 무지몽매의 시대로 규정함으로써 이슬람 발생 이전의 아랍 시대를 홀대했고, 이븐 할둔 등 이슬람 아랍 중동 내부자적 관점으로 역사를 다루는 역사가들에게도 지대한 영향을 미쳤다. 결국 아랍 민족의 역사는 이슬람이 발호한 7세기 이후의 역사서술로 흡수, 초기 서두가 간략 개괄되게 되었다.[3]

---

[1] 14세기 튀니스 출신의 이슬람 역사가, 사상가, 정치가. 당시 혼란했던 북아프리카의 정치, 사회에 대해 최초의 사회학적 견해를 가지고 정리했으며, 당시 전통적인 이슬람 역사관과 차별되는 객관적, 비판적인 분석을 통해 역사의 본질과 역사 변천 과정, 인류 역사 흐름의 일반 법칙을 조명하려 시도했다. 주요저서로는 무캇디마(Muqaddimah, 역사서설, 이슬람사상, 1377) 등이 있다.
송경근, 「이븐 칼둔의 아사비야에 대한 연구」, 『한국중동학회논총』 제36권 제3호, p.69-92, 2016.

[2] '무지'를 뜻하는 아랍어에서 유래. 이슬람이 등장하기 이전 시대, 상태.

[3] "과거 자힐리야의 삶과 무슬림이 된 이후의 삶 사이에는 명확한 단절이 있어야 한다. 자힐리야와의 관계를 완전히 끊어냈을 때 무슬림은 비로소 완전히 이슬람의 품 안에 들어가는 것이다.", 사이드 꾸틉, 서정민 역, 『진리를 향한 이정표(이슬람 원리주의 혁명의 실천적 지침서)』, 평사리, 2011, p.73

또한 버나드 루이스(Bernard Lewis), 한스 큉(Hans Kung) 등 서구에서 아랍 이슬람 사를 바라본 학문적 권위자들의 경우도, 라틴을 이은 헬라족이 세운 비잔틴 제국으로 대표되는 서구와 7세기 이후 아랍이 이슬람으로 종교체제화 된 뒤에 조우한 아랍 이슬람이 서구가 본격적으로 경험한 아랍이기에, 7세기 이슬람 이전의 아랍에 대해 간과된 측면이 크다하겠다.[4]

2 연구 제약을 넘어
– 아랍 유목문화 기록 부재와 헬라 지성에 수혈 받은 이슬람 지적 아카이브 활용

이처럼 아랍 역사 관점의 패러다임을 형성한 권위자들의 시각에서 서양, 중동 내부를 막론하고 아랍의 근원에 대해 간과된 측면이 크다. 또한 아랍은 이슬람 종교 체계화 이전에 유목민으로 살아온바 정주(定住)적 기록 문화가 약했

---

4 전완경, 『아랍문화사』, 한국학술정보, 2013, p.42

으며[5], 따라서 이슬람 체제 이전의 아랍에 대한 기록이 많지 않은 것도 아랍의 기원과 이슬람 이전의 역사에 대해 연구하기에 불리한 측면으로 작용한다. 그러나 이슬람은 구약과 신약의 내러티브를 차용해 간 꾸란의 내적 모순이 커, 성서의 내적 일관성과 통일성에 비견될 수 없는바, 이슬람 경전의 모순을 헬라 지성의 매개변증으로 메우려한 측면이 있다. 이것은 아이러니하게도 이슬람 사회에 헬라지성 수혈의 길을 열어 아랍 지중해권의 각종 도서관, 아카데미 건립 등을 통해 지적 축적을 가져오기도 했다.[6] 따라서 아랍의 비교적 정확한 구전 구술 문화와 이슬람 이후 헬라 조우를 통해, 아랍 사회에 체계적으로 남아 있는 지적 아카이브를 활용해 아랍의 기원과 개론, 이슬람 이전 역사에 관해 학문적 패러다임을 새로이 열 수 있는 현장 연구가(硏究家), 이론가이자 동시에 선교사인 자원이 학문적 체계화에 도전해 보면 좋겠다. 아랍의 기원과 이슬람 이전에 역사 영역은 중동의 실체를 파악하는 데 매우 긴요하면서도 강력한 통찰력을 제공할 터이나 앞서 말한 연유 때문에 학문적 연구 영역으로도 거의 손대지 않은

---

5 전완경, 위의 책 p.18~20.

6 브리태니커 편찬위원회, 『브리태니커 필수 교양사전 이슬람』, 아고라, 2017, p.74~85

무주공산에 가깝다. 중동 아랍에 관해 막대한 학문적 연구가 고대 중세로부터 현대까지 이어져 왔으나, 이 영역은 개척의 연구 영역으로 남아 연구 성과가 입증된다면 학문적 패러다임과 새로운 틀을 열만한 분야일 것이다.

3 성경에서 본 아랍의 기원
– 이스마엘과 무함마드로 이어지는 아랍인 계보

의외롭게도 아랍인들은 사우디아라비아를 중심으로 한 남부 아랍인을 '카흐탄(Qahtan)'이라 명명하면서도 그들을 이스마엘과 무함마드를 잇는, 혈통적·영적 적통으로 말하지 않는다. 오히려 북부 아랍인들을 '아드난(Adnan)'이라 명명하면서 그들을 이스마엘과 무함마드를 이은 혈통적·영적 적통으로 말한다.[7] 구약을 통해 이스마엘이 아브라함 가계에서 쫓겨나 이집트 출신인 하갈이 이집트의 경계에서 길을 잃어 아라비아로 남하한 것은 자명하다.[8] 그런데 왜 북부 아랍

---

7 전완경, 위의 책, p.22~25

8 그가 바란 광야에 거주할 때에 그의 어머니가 그를 위하여 애굽 땅에서 아내를 얻어 주었더라(창 21:21)

인을 아랍인 스스로 이스마엘-무함마드를 이은 혈통적 직계라 생각하는 것일까? 일반적으로 아랍인들은 어느 가문, 누구의 아들로 이름이 표기될 정도로 혈연적 계통이 명확히 전승되어왔으며 결국 그 근원적 연유는 성경까지 올라가 아랍인의 조상, 이스마엘 가문과 에서의 결혼에서 답을 찾을 수 있다. 성경에서 보면 북부 아랍인의 정체와 근원이 나오는데 아랍인의 시조 이스마엘의 딸이 에서와 결혼한 일이 기록되어 있다.(창25:13, 28:9)[9] 또한 북부에서 이스마엘의 차자, 게달 계통 등의 자손도 번성하여 아라비아와 함께 열거된다.(사60:6-7, 겔27:20-22)[10]

그리하여 북부 아랍인이 이 계통에서 형성되었는데 오

---

9 이스마엘의 아들들의 이름은 그 이름과 그 세대대로 이와 같으니라 이스마엘의 장자는 느바욧이요 그 다음은 게달과 앗브엘과 밉삼과(창25:13) 이에 에서가 이스마엘에게 가서 그 본처들 외에 아브라함의 아들 이스마엘의 딸이요 느바욧의 누이인 마할랏을 아내로 맞이하였더라(창28:9)

10 허다한 낙타, 미디안과 에바의 어린 낙타가 네 가운데에 가득할 것이며 스바 사람들은 다 금과 유향을 가지고 와서 여호와의 찬송을 전파할 것이며, 게달의 양 무리는 다 네게로 모일 것이요 느바욧의 숫양은 네게 공급되고 내 제단에 올라 기꺼이 받음이 되리니 내가 내 영광의 집을 영화롭게 하리라(사60:6-7)
드단은 네 상인이 되었음이여 말을 탈 때 까는 천을 너와 거래하였도다. 아라비아와 게달의 모든 고관은 네 손아래 상인이 되어 어린 양과 숫양과 염소들, 그것으로 너와 거래하였도다. 스바와 라아마의 상인들도 너의 상인들이 됨이여 각종 극상품 향 재료와 각종 보석과 황금으로 네 물품을 바꾸어 갔도다(겔27:20-22)

늘날 요르단, 레바논, 시리아, 팔레스타인 등지에서 볼 수 있고, 이 북부 계통 아랍인 중에서 이슬람을 창시한 무함마드가 나왔다. 따라서 이스마엘-무함마드를 잇는 혈통적 계보는 사우디아라비아의 남부 아랍인에 근거하지 않고 북부 아랍인임을 오늘날에 아랍 사회도 인정하는 바다.

4 아랍의 기원 연구와 아랍학, 중동학, 이슬람학 개론 상 연구 범주 재정립
– 북아프리카권, 중앙아시아권, 동남아시아권까지

아랍의 기원이 성서에서 근거한 바, 이스마엘 느바욧의 딸과 에서의 혼인과 이스마엘의 다른 아들들 게달 계통 등에 발달해, 통칭 북부 아랍인의 형성되어 무함마드 계보에 이르기까지, 혈통적 아랍에 계보와 이슬람을 연 창시자의 계열까지 연유를 찾을 수 있겠다. 이러한 아랍의 기원과 이슬람의 발생에 이르는 계통적 아랍을 구분하면 그간 아랍 이슬람의 영향을 받은 많은 지역의 학문적 연구개론 카테고리에 재정립 필요성을 생각하게 된다. 크게 아랍 이슬람에 영향을 받았던 지역 등은 물론 중동, 북아프리카, 중앙아시아, 동남아시아 등지 이다. 그럼에도 이들을 연구하는 학문 연구 범위와 그 구분을 나누는 기준은 아랍 혈통에 의한 것인지, 언어적 호환성에 따른 것인지, 이슬람 종교 정신성에 입각한 것인지, 지정학적 위치에 따른 것인지 모호했다.

중동이라는 개념은 근동이라는 서구 중심 지정학적 개념에 반발하여 나온 개념이다. 따라서 아랍과 이슬람이 발호한 핵심 지역임에도 중동학, 중동권이라는 말은 아랍 이슬람의 특성을 담기에는 불명확한 지정학적 개념일 뿐이다.[11]

우선 혈통적, 민족적 아랍은 전술했다시피 이스마엘과 무함마드에 이르는 계보의 직계를 중심으로 북부 아랍과 남부 아랍으로 나뉜다. 여기서 혈연적 직계는 북부 아랍이나 이슬람이 메카, 메디나를 중심으로 남부 아라비아에서 발호했다는 점과 여전히 이슬람 종교 구심력이 사우디아라비아에서 작동된다는 점에서 아랍의 7세기 이후 종교 정신성에 입

---

11 인남식(국립외교원 교수), 2022.
https://www.youtube.com/watch?v=FHcm7B_VjVE

각한 아랍의 핵심은 사우디아라비아의 남부 아랍이다.[12]

그렇다면 북아프리카 아랍과 중앙아시아, 동남아시아 이슬람권 연구 범위를 나누는 기준은 과연 중동처럼 지정학적 개념으로 구분된 것인가? 아랍이라는 개념에 혈연적 민족적 단위로 구분한 것인가? 아니면 이슬람이라는 종교정신성을 기준으로 나눈 것인가? 기준이 모호하다. 북아프리카는 이슬람의 영향을 받아 북아프리카 '아랍'이라는 개념으로 두리뭉실하게 통술하면서도, 중앙아시아 역시 이슬람에 영향을 받은 지역임에도 중앙아시아 '아랍'이라는 말이나 학문적 연구 범위로 통술하거나 개념화하지 않는다. 그렇다면 북아프리카 권역이 이슬람의 영향을 받았다고 해서 혈통적, 민족적 아랍인가? 남부, 북부 아랍인처럼 혈통적 연관성이 북아프리카 민족에 거의 없는데도 북아프리카 '아랍'이라는 단어를 쓰는 이유는 무엇인가? 따져보면 사실상 북아프리카 '아랍'은 언어적 호환성으로 구분된 개념이다. 현재 북아프리카권은 이슬람화 된 뒤에 중앙아시아와 다르게 현재도 공시적

---

12 전완경, 위의 책, p.33-34

아랍어를 사용, 통용하는 지역이다.[13] 그래서 북아프리카 '아랍'권의 '아랍'은 혈연적, 부족적, 민족적, 종교 정신적인 구분 개념이라기보다 아랍어라는 공시 언어 호환성에 따른 구분 기준인 셈이다.

한편 중앙아시아와 동남아시아는 이슬람의 영향으로 꾸란이 아랍어로 보급되어 문자 아랍어의 영향권 하에 있기도 하나, 북아프리카처럼 아랍어를 자신들의 통용 언어로까지 받아들이지는 않았다. 그래서 중앙아시아 '아랍', 동남아시아 '아랍'이라는 개념은 북아프리카 '아랍'처럼 통용되지 않는다.

결론적으로 중동, 아랍, 이슬람, 북아프리카 아랍, 중앙아시아 동남아시아 이슬람 연구에는 좀 더 정밀하고 일관된 학문적 연구 범위와 범주 구분 기준이 필요하다. 이렇게 학문적 연구 범위가 지정학적 개념, 언어적 개념, 혈통적·민족적 개념, 종교적 개념이 뒤섞여 학문적 합의 기준이 없는 연구 분야도 드물다. 성서에서 비롯된 아랍의 기원에 관한 연구가 간과되거나 미진한 채로 7세기 이후 이슬람 발호와 서구와 조우하는 지정학적 영향 등으로만 기술되어 그렇다고 보여진

---

[13] 모로코의 한 대학교수는 "아랍주의는 본질적으로 언어와 문화"라고 주장한다. 전완경, 위의 책, p.36

다. 첫 단추가 애매모호하게 끼워진 셈이다.

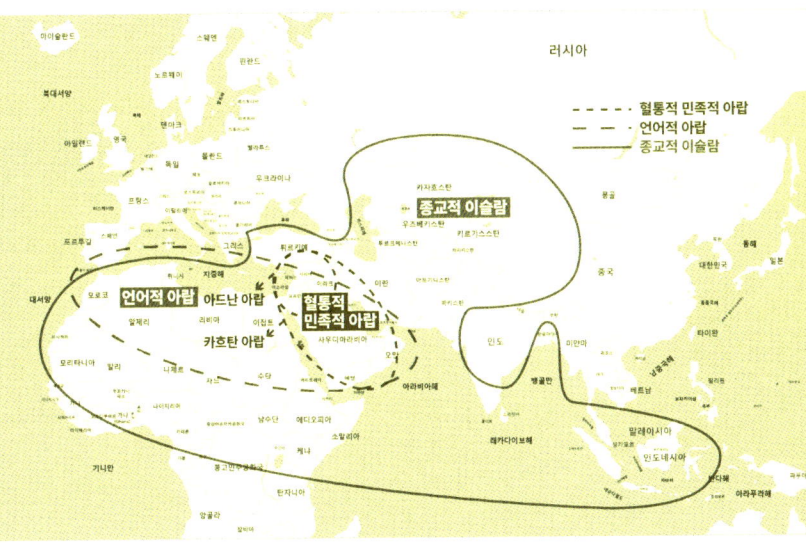

5 아랍 근원 부족주의와 무함마드, 그리고 이스라엘 하마스 전쟁과 평화 해법

최근에 서구권을 중심으로 이스라엘 하마스 전쟁을 바라보면서 연방론이 새롭게 제시되었다. 기존 국제사회의 해법으로 제시되었던 이스라엘 팔레스타인 두 국가 해법[14], 이스라엘 중심에 일 국가 일 체제론[15]이 대두되어왔으나 현실화되기 난망했으니 미국처럼 이스라엘과 팔레스타인의 각 자립을 인정하면서 느슨한 연방 국가를 구성하면 어떠하겠냐는 제의다. 일 국가론이 완전한 결혼이고, 두 개 국가론이 이혼이면, 연방 국가론[16]은 마치 합의 동거와 같다는 예시를 들며 국제사회에 호소된 견해이다. 그러나 이런 시각은 엄연히 서구체제의 모티브를 차용할 뿐 중동 일대와 아랍 사회의 근원과 특수성을 잘 모르고서 아전인수(我田引水)격으로 이 극한의 대립을 풀어보려는 시도이다.

왜냐하면 중동 아랍 이스라엘 갈등의 근원을 형성한 이

---

[14] Two-state solution, 유대민족을 위한 이스라엘과 팔레스타인 민족을 위한 팔레스타인을 설립함으로 이스라엘과 팔레스타인 분쟁을 해결하기 위한 제안으로 1993년 오슬로협정(Oslo Accords)의 일환이다.
브리태니커, https://www.britannica.com/topic/two-state-solution

[15] One state solution, 유세프 무나이에(예루살렘기금 팔레스타인 센터 사무총장)는 '팔레스타인 사람에게 동등한 권리를 보장하는 헌법을 제정하고 진상조사와 보상을 통해 과거사를 극복하고 단일 국가를 세우자'고 주장했다. 포린어페어스(Foreign Affairs), 2019.

[16] 서안 지구 7개 주요 부족들이 UAE식의 연방을 구성해 국제사회가 건국을 지원하는 케다르 플랜(여덟 국가 해법)도 있다. 인남식, 2018.

스마엘과 이삭의 고대 갈등[17]은 사실은 중동에 부족주의의 원한과 원수맺음에 근거한 '눈에는 눈, 이에는 이' 고대 중동 율법과 그 유전이 대대로 중동 내부에서 흘러 내려 전하여 져오기 때문이다. 이는 이슬람이 체계화되기 전 중동 아랍의 뿌리에 근거한 유전이나 무함마드조차 이런 프로토타입(prototype)의 아랍의 부족주의를 극복하지 못했다. 무함마드는 유일신 사상으로 부족주의를 통합한 이슬람 이전에 부족 갈등과 분열 사회 양상을 자힐리야라 했으나, 무함마드조차 아랍 부족주의의 원한관계로부터 자유로울 수 없었다. 메카에서 메디나로 이주 당시 선지자를 자처한 자신을 무시했던 아랍 유대인들을 원한 관계로 보복, 무참히 학살하고 그 부녀자들을 노예 삼아 부리다가 그들의 원한으로 독살당한 것이 무함마드의 생애의 끝이었다.

따라서 '눈에는 눈, 이에는 이'에 중동 아랍의 율법 유전 전통은 오늘날에 아랍을 해석하는데 근간이 된다. 이스라엘 하마스 전쟁 간 이스라엘과 하마스, 팔레스타인, 아랍 이슬람 사회 간 극한 대립을 나이브하게 단순 서구렌즈로 투과해

---

[17] 사라가 본즉 아브라함의 아들 애굽 여인 하갈의 아들이 이삭을 놀리는지라. 그가 아브라함에게 이르되 이 여종과 그 아들을 내쫓으라 이 종의 아들은 내 아들 이삭과 함께 기업을 얻지 못하리라 하므로(창 21:9–10)

체제 구조로 해석하는 것은 아랍의 뿌리를 간과해서이다. 아랍 부족주의의 은원관계는 체제나 정부, 종교보다 우선적이며 근원적이다. 따라서 이스라엘 하마스 간 전쟁은 부족주의에 입각한 원한을 짙게 할 뿐, 체제나 거버넌스 구조, 국제기구의 견제와 제안을 통해 해결될 수 없고, 오직 율법의 요구를 이기고 완성한 용서의 복음과 화해의 소식만으로 평화가 가능하다 하겠다.

6 아랍 이슬람 부족주의로 조명해 본 중동소요사태[18]

1) 리비아 내전의 원인 – 이슬람 부족주의

독재자 카다피[19]의 최후는 참혹했다. 리비아의 카다피는

---

18 이하 글은 중동 소요 사태가 일어난 2011년 직후에 쓰였다.

19 리비아의 국가원수로 2011년을 기준으로 세계 최장인 42년 동안 리비아를 통치했던 독재자. 2011년 2월 15일 리비아 제2의 도시인 벵가지에서 발생한 반정부 민주화 시위에서 시작해 부족간 갈등으로 번지며 수많은 희생자를 낳은 리비아혁명이 10월 20일 카다피가 사망함으로써 막을 내리게 된다.

왕 중의 왕이라는 호칭을 즐겨 사용했는데 이는 고대의 부족 할거시대에 혼란을 마감한 왕들이 자신을 지칭하는 표현이다.[20] 카다피는 왕이라는 다소 시대착오적인 호칭을 즐기며 절대 권력에 군림했지만 결국 부족들 사이의 원한으로 인해 희생되었다. 중동 소요 사태를 민주화로 규정하며 개입하는 서구는 자가당착적이고 아전인수격인 과오를 저지르고 있다. 서구적 민주화 모델링을 중동사회의 대규모 소요의 원인과 결과로 받아들이며 힘과 패권으로 개입하는 것도 자가당착이려니와, 중동에 대한 이해와 도식도 매우 자기중심적이고 단선적이다. 그리고 이러한 행태는 오랜 세월 중동과 서구 대립의 비극의 씨앗이 되어왔다.[21]

독재자 카다피가 축출되고도 끝까지 그를 추종하는 일부 리비아인들의 미련스러운 충정이나, 이와 대조적으로 카

---

[20] 2009년 UN 총회에서 카다피는 연설 중에 스스로를 '아프리카의 왕 중 왕(King of Kings of Africa)'으로 지칭했다.
Africanews with United Nations, "Muammar Gaddafi at the 64th UN General Assembly in 2009", Africanews, 2019.09.12., https://www.africanews.com/2017/09/19/speech-muammar-gaddafi-at-the-64th-un-general-assembly-in-2009/

[21] 인남식, 「국제정치의 이상을 좌초시킨 아랍의 봄」, 『아랍의 봄 그 후 10년의 흐름』, 서울대학교출판문화원, 2022, p.247-250.

다피의 엄청난 은닉재산으로 회유 받고도, 이미 권좌에서 쫓겨난 그를 끝까지 추격해 참혹하게 살육했던 또 다른 한편의 리비아인들이 보인 극단적 광기의 차이를 단순히 서구적 민주화의 열망 정도로만 해석하고 이해할 수 있을까?[22] 독재자 카다피를 옹호하려는 집단과 축출하려는 집단 사이에서 리비아인들끼리의 내전을 그저 종교나 정치, 민족 이데올로기가 잉태한 체제 대립 정도에 대입할 수 있을까? 의도적인 체제(System) 이전에 자연 발생적 부족(Tribe)이 있었다. 부족이라는 개념은 오늘날 서구적 헤게모니가 종교, 정치, 경제가 결집된 하나의 체제로 등장하기 훨씬 이전에 자연적으로 발생한 것이었다. 그래서 부족적 할거는 현대의 시간에서 펼쳐지는 양상이라고 하는 것보다는 고대 코드적인 것으로 보는 것이 타당하다. 왜냐하면, 집중적인 힘의 양상을 지니는 체제가 힘을 결집하여 분산적, 할거적 양상을 지니는 부족을 제압해 압도적으로 승리하는 것은 다분히 서구적이고 현대적인 양상이기 때문이다.[23]

---

[22] 휴먼라이츠워치(Human Rights Watch, 국제인권감시기구) https://www.hrw.org/report/2012/10/16/death-dictator/bloody-vengeance-sirte

[23] 에이미 추아, 김승진 역, 『정치적 부족주의』, 부키, 2020, p.79-81.

아랍 이슬람은 역사적으로 부족과 종교 체제의 경계 사이, 교착지점의 산물이다. 무함마드[24]의 생전 AD 7세기 이전에 아라비아 반도는 중동 패권 중심에서 그저 변방에 지나지 않았다. 당시 중동의 형편은 기독교의 자양분을 먹어치운 빈 그릇처럼, 문명의 나이로는 이미 노쇠한 동로마 제국과 옛 제국의 전성기를 향한 부활의 욕망이 꿈틀대지만, 기독교의 정신성과 같은 깊은 종교적 자양분이 부족한 페르시아 제국과의 끊임없는 충돌이 지루하게 이어지고 있었다.[25] 이러한 파괴적인 에너지는 인류 공동체에 새로운 역동성을 부여하지는 못했지만, 힘을 연동시켜 패권의 법칙을 따르게 하는 제국적인 체제의 대결이 되었다. 그리고 동시대에는 이들을 대항할 세력이나 문명적 대안이 없는 것처럼 보였다.

무함마드는 이러한 중동 근방의 폐단적인 문명 충돌 상황 속에서 아라비아 반도를 재편하고자 유일신 사상과 아랍 중심의 사회 질서를 가지고 분연히 일어났다. 중동 근방에는 노쇠한 문명의 힘들이 충돌하고 있었지만, 원시적 아라비아

---

24 이슬람교도는 보통 알 라술(al-Rasul, 전령자), 라술 알라(Rasul Allah), 즉 '알라의 사도'라고 부른다. 이슬람교의 창시자이다.

25 브리태니커 편찬위원회(2017), 앞의 책, p.107-111.

반도 내부는 부족 사회의 반목과 불화의 연속이었다. 아라비아 반도의 지나치게 극단적인 부족주의 세계관은 근친관계나 부족적인 친화력이 있는 집단끼리는 폐쇄적일 정도로 구심력과 결속력이 강했지만, 배타적인 집단과는 한번 불화와 반목이 진행되면 부족 대대로 원수가 되었다.[26]

무함마드는 상인으로서 원거리 거래를 자주 다녔는데, 그때 접하게 된 유일신 관념과 아라비아 내부에 유입되어 온 비주류 기독교인들, 디아스포라[27] 유대인들과 교류하면서 그들을 통해 접한 구약의 성경 내러티브[28]에 매료되었다. 그는 아라비아 부족 사회 내부의 끊임없는 은원관계에 따른 혼란과 반목의 요인을 종교적 불경건 때문이라 지적하면서, 다양한 부족의 다양한 우상들을 배제할 것을 촉구했다. 부족의 갈등과 아라비아 반도의 혼란과 반목, 끊임없는 부족적 분쟁 상황의 원인을 다신 숭배로 인한 분열과 저주로 지목하면서

---

[26] 브리태니커 편찬위원회(2017), 앞의 책, p.34-42.

[27] 원래 유대인의 민족적 이산(離散) 상황을 뜻하는 용어였지만, 현대에서는 전쟁과 식민지화로 고국을 등져야 했던 난민이나 인민 그리고 그 후손들을 총칭하는 단어로 확장되어 쓰이고 있다.

[28] '말하다'라는 뜻의 라틴어 동사 Narrare에서 유래한 단어로 스토리텔링과 유사한 의미를 가진다. 실화나 허구의 사건들을 묘사하는 것, 그 자체뿐만 아니라 이야기를 조직하고 전개하기 위해 이용되는 각종 전략이나 형식 등을 포괄하는 개념으로 사용된다.

유일신 사상을 통해 부족 간에 경계를 허물고 아라비아 반도의 통합을 구축하고자 했던 것이다.

그러나 무함마드 자신도 기독교와 유대교의 유일신 관념과 부정확한 성경 정보를 차용했을 뿐 부족적 가치관과 영향력으로부터 자유롭지는 못했다. 그조차도 자신을 이단적인 자칭 선지자로 취급하는 아라비아 내 디아스포라 유대 부족에게 모멸감을 느끼고 전쟁 중에 항복한 그들을 무참히 살육, 멸족시켰다. 한 번은 멸족당한 유대 족속의 여인 하나가 무함마드에게 음식을 대접하는 척하며 그가 좋아하는 양고기에 독을 발라 내어놓았고, 무심결에 이를 먹던 무함마드가 이상한 맛을 느끼고 음식을 뱉어 가까스로 목숨을 구한 사건이 있었다. 그 뒤로 그는 평생 자신의 몸이 아플 때마다, 생의 마지막 순간에 질병으로 죽어갈 때조차, 자신의 쇠락을 독살 미수 사건 때문으로 돌렸다. 평생을 독살 미수 사건에 대한 원한으로 살았던 것이다. 사실 무함마드는 유일신 알라 사상에 적대적이지만 않으면 부족적 관습을 그대로 답습하거나 거의 용인하기도 했다.[29]

무함마드가 이슬람 종교와 부족통합이라는 명분으로

---

[29] 브리태니커 편찬위원회(2017), 앞의 책, p.45-50.

중동전역을 무력으로 제패하면서, 이슬람은 그의 부족적 관습이 그대로 반영된 토양 위에 종교체제로서 세워졌고, 지금도 중동 전역에 고스란히 안착해있다. 이슬람은 마치 세월의 이끼가 켜켜이 쌓인 것처럼 구심력이 강하며, 동일한 가치관과 획일적인 라이프스타일로 구성원들을 재편해 온 여타의 종교체제, 정치체제, 경제체제들과 상반된 차이를 가지게 되었다. 이슬람은 중동 전역을 하나의 종교체제로 구축하면서도 할거적이고 배타적인 부족주의[30]를 허용하고 독려했는데, 이슬람과 다른 여타 체제들은 대부분 부족주의와 적대적이어서 공존하기보다는 극단적으로 혹은 점진적으로 해체하는 방식을 취했다.

예컨대 중앙집권적 정치체제를 구축하는 왕이 부족적 할거를 불편해하는 것은 뻔한 이치다. 단일의 믿음과 가톨릭 양식을 고수하는 교황이 부족적 혈연관계의 폐쇄성을 기뻐하지 않았던 것이다. 효율적 경제체제를 신봉하는 자들과 그

---

30 일반적으로 동질적인 전통과 조상, 언어, 문화, 종교 등을 가진 사람들의 집단을 추구하는 이념이다. 소규모이고 상대적으로 고립되어 있으며 정치적 통합의 정도가 낮은 상태를 이상으로 한다. 중앙집권화된 정치권력이 존재하지 않는 부족제를 목표로 하고 있는 경우가 대부분이다.

것을 뒷받침하는 경제 이론가들은 예측 가능하며 도식화 할 수 있는 경제 현상을 통해 생산과 분배에 일반적이고 경제적인 구심력을 창출하기 원했다. 그들은 부족마다 자급자족적인 다양한 양태에 관한 관심이 적었다. 또한, 중동 이슬람의 부족주의와 체제 교차점은 아프리카의 고대 원시 부족과도, 서구의 합리적인 체제와도 다르다. 리비아의 내전에 대한 이해는 이러한 아랍 이슬람의 내적 토양에 대한 이해로부터 시작되어야 한다. 사실 왕처럼 군림했던 카다피에 대한 적대 부족의 저항이 추동력이 되었기에 민의를 통한 리비아 독재체제 전복이 가능했다. 부족의 가문과 명예가 국가법보다 중요시되는 아랍인들에게 하물며 절대 권력의 카다피라도 부족의 적대세력이라면 타협의 여지가 없이 원수가 되었기 때문이다. 카다피가 잔인하게 살육된 이유는 물론 그의 폭정에서 일차적 원인을 찾아야 하지만, 부족적 대립 양상에 따른 리비아 상황을 이해하지 않고는 온전한 진단을 내릴 수 없다.[31]

현재 리비아는 위험한 도전에 직면해 있다. 물론 카다피가 위험인물이긴 했지만, 그의 축출을 대신할 마땅한 중앙권위나 권력이 존재하지 않는 상태에서 부족 집단마다 무기와

---

[31] 브리태니커 편찬위원회(2017), 앞의 책, p.434-438.

무력이 주어졌다. 그들은 고대 코드로부터 내려온 가문중심의 은원 관계에 따라 행동할 것이다. 또한, 체제가 등장해도 자신들의 부족적 입지를 강화하는 방향으로 체제를 인정하려 할 것이다. 그러나 리비아에는 여러 기원과 처지가 다른 많은 부족들이 상존해 있고 이 부족들의 다양한 요구를 모두 성취할 정부는 존재하지 않을 것이다. 따라서 체제를 안정시키려 해도 당분간 부족적 할거와 갈등의 양상이 리비아를 지배할 것이다. 혼란과 내전으로 치닫지 않도록 기도할 일이다.[32]

2) 아랍 민주화 혁명의 역설, 서구의 개입과 중동 독재 체제 극단화의 상승 작용

---

[32] 유엔 인권위원회의 보고서에 따르면 리비아는 유엔이 인정한 과도정부인 리비아통합정부(GNU)는 서부를, 군벌 리비아국민군(LNA)는 동부를 나눠 통치하는 불안정한 정치 구조로 무장 민병대들이 할거하여 경쟁하고 있다. 특히 이주민들과 난민들에 대한 납치, 살인 등의 범죄가 횡행하며 최악의 인권상황에 직면해 있다.(2023년 3월27일)
Mustafa Fetouri, "Libya's human rights situation is worse than what it was under Gaddafi", MIDDLE EAST MONITOR, 2023.04.13, https://www.middleeastmonitor.com/20230413-libyas-human-rights-situation-is-worse-than-what-it-was-under-gaddafi/

이러한 중동 전역의 소요 사태를 포괄적인 '민주화 혁명'으로 규정하려는 시도가 있었다. 서구적인 관점과 합의로 볼 때, 튀니지로부터 촉발된 민의적 봉기는 아랍 전역의 독재적 권위에 대한 괄목할 만한 민주화 과정의 도전일 수 있겠다. 소요와 봉기의 과정조차 정파적 조직이 구심력을 가지거나 대항 엘리트층을 중심으로 일어난 것이 아닌, 소셜 네트워크 서비스(Social Network Service)[33]라는 새로운 소통 구조를 통해 자발적인 형태로 추진됐다는 점에서 서구는 자신들 근대의 태동점이라 규정하는 프랑스대혁명에 비견하고 있는 듯하다.

그러나 역설적이게도 봉기의 원인부터 결말까지 자세히 고찰해보면 아랍 사회의 서구를 향한 뿌리 깊은 불신과 피해의식이 곳곳에서 감지된다. 알다시피 튀니지 소요의 시작은 길거리에 내어 쫓긴 아랍 청년층의 경제적 막다른 골목에서 시작되었다.[34] 내부적으로 아랍 정치의 무능, 특히 왕정과 군부, 종교적 독재체제가 이슬람 내부에 부패와 국민에게는 고

---

33 온라인의 가상공간을 통해 인맥을 쌓고, 정보를 공유하는 인터넷 기반의 커뮤니티 서비스를 총칭한다.

34 엄한진, 「튀니지, 아랍의 봄의 트리거」, 『아랍의 봄 그 후 10년의 흐름』, 서울대학교출판문화원, 2022, p.4-6.

단함을 가져 왔지만, 이슬람은 종교적 자부심과 서구에 대한 뿌리 깊은 적개심으로 인하여 그 책임을 외부로 돌려왔으며 앞으로도 그럴 가능성이 커 보인다. 또한, 서구 대 비서구의 경제적 불평등은 서구의 헤게모니와 서구가 추진한 세계화에 따른 경제 구조적 부작용에 따른 것임을 부인할 수 없다. 그렇다면 결과적으로 소요 사태를 통해 국가적 변동을 경험한 나라들인 튀니지, 이집트, 리비아 등을 보자. 이들 나라는 내부적으로 독재체제를 구가하였는지는 몰라도 서구에 대해 어떠한 이유에서건 친서구는 아니더라도 개방적 출구 정도는 열어놓은 국가였으며, 내부적 소요와 불만이 확산될 수 있었던 사우디아라비아와 이란 등 중동 내에 극단적 독재체제를 구축한 나라들은 오히려 철저한 통제 속에 중동 소요 사태를 관리할 수 있었다.[35]

이러한 결과 앞에 중동 내 폐쇄적이고 극단적인 종교 왕정군부독재체제를 갖춘 나라들은 서구체제에 대한 경멸과 경계가 깊어졌다. 서구 민주화 모델이 이식되기는커녕 서구에 대한 커넥션 자체를 위험한 것으로 간주할 가능성이 커진

---

35 구기연, 「이란, 미완의 혁명과 시민 불복종 운동」, 『아랍의 봄 그 후 10년의 흐름』, 서울대학교출판문화원, 2022, p.208.

것이다. 왜냐하면, 서구가 민주화와 패권이라는 야누스적 행태로 언제든지 자신들과 교류와 커넥션이 있는 중동국가들의 내부적 소요를 이용해 혼란을 가중할 가능성을 보여 왔기 때문이다.[36]

역사적 축적은 일시적 시의성을 훨씬 뛰어넘는 거대한 힘이기에 중동 소요 사태를 관망하면서 시의적 분절을 통해서만 사건을 읽는 것은 다분히 오판의 가능성을 불러올 수 있다. 역사적으로 서구와 중동의 갈등은 어떤 전쟁이나 충돌보다도 가장 뿌리 깊고 거대한 크기의 증오로 얼룩져 있다. 고대의 성경 기록이 증거하는 아브라함 가계의 이삭과 이스마엘의 갈등과 반목이 서구와 중동의 정신적 근원의 충돌이라는 것은 심각한 예언이다.[37] 고대 코드의 기록이 역사 전체를 지배하는 주요 핵심코드가 될 줄 누가 감히 짐작했을까? 사실상 현대를 살아가는 공동체에 지난 한 세기 동안 가장 큰 정신적 후유증을 가져왔던 냉전 기간, 즉 백 년 간 내려온 이데올로기 갈등은 이삭과 이스마엘의 역사적 갈등에 비하면 역사적 길이와 충격 면에서 매우 미미한 상처인 셈이다. 가깝

---

36 에이미 추아(2020), 앞의 책, p.107-110.

37 그가 사람 중에 들나귀 같이 되리니 그의 손이 모든 사람을 치겠고 모든 사람의 손이 그를 칠지며 그가 모든 형제와 대항해서 살리라 하니라(창세기 16:12)

게는 이스라엘과 아랍의 갈등, 제 1, 2차 세계 대전을 통한 서구의 지배와 억압, 유럽 대 튀르크의 대결, 십자군 전쟁, 헬라와 페르시아 제국의 대립 등 이슬람교를 수입한 중동 사람들에게 수천 년 동안 서구는 타협할 수 없는 적대 세력이었다. 그렇기에 대부분의 중동국가에 서구의 개입은 불행한 기억으로 각인되어 있다. 아랍의 왕정 종교의 군부 독재자들이 폐쇄적 시스템을 지속해서 운영할 수 있는 이유는 국민이 그들에게 절대적 지지를 보내서라기보다는 서구 외세의 개입에 대한 반사 이익의 결과라고 볼 수 있다.[38] 그런 면에서 튀니지, 이집트, 리비아의 독재체제 붕괴로 서구 민주화 체제가 이식되고 있다는 발상은 순진한 생각이다. 중동 내에 대책 없는 절대적 독재 시스템을 구가하고 있는 사우디아라비아, 이란 등의 종교. 정치 집권자들은 서구에 대한 적개심을 다시금 확인하고 노골적으로 백성들에게 학습시킬 것이다. 이라크와 리비아, 이집트 등을 둘러싼 혼란은 서구 세력의 개입과

---

[38] 이란의 민족주의 지도자인 총리 무함마드 모사데크는 이란 민심에 힘입어 1951년 석유를 국유화 한다. 이에 이권을 빼앗긴 영국 MI6와 미국 CIA가 모사데크를 축출했고, 이후 이에 반발한 반외세주의가 이슬람 종교지도자들과 합세해 1979년 이란 이슬람 혁명을 성공해, 최고 종교지도자가 종신 집권하는 신정체제를 이뤘다. 박현도(서강대 유로메나연구소), 2023.
https://www.youtube.com/watch?v=2Rl5Xa071mw

내부 추동이 자신들의 권좌와 나라에 큰 혼란과 불행을 일으킬 수 있는 위험한 접촉임을 주장하며 내부 단속과 폐쇄성을 정당화할 것이다.

그렇다면, 중동권 민심의 분출구 역할을 하는 청년들이 서구에 우호적이며 무분별한 추종을 보인 것일까? 답은 간단치 않다. 엘리트들이라면 세계화 메커니즘의 부작용에 따른 제삼 세계의 경제적 피해를 인지할 것이고, 중동 역사를 지식적, 경험적으로 물려받은 이들이라면 서구에 대해 우호적일 가능성이 별로 없다. 새로운 체제가 안정된다면 그들은 서구와의 커넥션을 불편해할 소지가 다분하다. 물론 서구는 자신들의 입장과 이익을 대변해 줄 누군가를 찾아 중동 신흥세력에 끊임없이 회유하고 야합하는 밀월관계를 요청하겠지만 그들의 대중동 정책은 언제나 그런 식으로 진정한 신뢰를 얻는 것에 실패해 왔다.

3) 예멘, 이집트, 리비아 독재와 이슬람 극단주의 세력

독재를 옹호할 생각은 추호도 없지만, 이슬람 극단주의가 가지는 폭력적 투쟁 양상을 볼 때 중동의 왕정, 군부 등의 독재는 불가피하게 이슬람 극단주의의 발흥을 억제한 측면이 있다.

이슬람 극단주의 세력은 종교적 신념에 따른다는 점에서 그 폭력의 정당화 양상이 극단적이다. 쿠데타로 군부 독재 정권을 열었던 나세르[39]가 젊은 날 한때 무슬림 형제단이라는 극단주의 세력에 관심을 보이고 그들의 활동의 반사 효과와 공조를 통해 이집트 정권을 장악했지만, 그는 곧 이슬람 극단주의 세력의 위험성을 알고 그들을 탄압했다. 이슬람 극단주의 세력인 무슬림 형제단으로부터 암살을 당할 뻔한 나세르는 이슬람 극단주의가 다른 정치체제와 타협하는 세력이 아니라는 것을 알았다. 그것은 철저한 탄압이었고 언제 암살당할지 모르는 생사의 문제였다. 나세르의 정치적 동지이자, 군부정권을 함께 열었던 사다트[40] 대통령은 이슬람

---

[39] 반둥회의(아시아—아프리카회의)에 출석하여 적극적인 중립주의·비동맹주의 외교정책을 추진했고 수에즈운하의 국유화 선언 후 수에즈전쟁이 일어났으나 국제여론의 지지로 이를 해결해 아시아·아프리카의 지도자가 되었다.

[40] 이스라엘과의 평화 없이는 이집트의 재건이 없다고 생각하고 이스라엘에 압력을 행사할 수 있는 미국에 접근하여 중동평화에 미국을 관여시키는 데 성공하였다. 현실주의적으로, 1977년 이스라엘을 방문하고 중동평화의 길을 닦았다.

신앙기조를 국민에게 보여주기 위해 무슬림 형제단에 대해 유화책과 압박책을 번갈아 썼지만 결국 그들에게 암살당했다. 이후 등장한 무바라크[41] 독재 정권에 가열찬 압박을 받은 무슬림 형제단은 폭력적 노선을 철회하다시피 했지만, 포스트 무바라크로 무슬림 형제단이 가장 유력한 정치세력으로 등장하면서 그들이 집권한다면 이집트는 그들의 극단적 폭력 노선이 부활할지 경계해야 하는 처지에 놓였다. 그들의 폭력적 노선 회귀를 견제할 수 있는 이집트 세력은 군부가 유일할 뿐이다.[42]

리비아의 왕 중의 왕이라 칭했던 카다피는 부족적 할거라는 리비아의 정치적 분열 양상을 독재를 통해 컨트롤했다. 그는 서구에 대해서 괴팍하리만큼 유연한 지도자였다. 때로는 서구에 대해 폭력적으로 대항하고, 이익이 된다면 안면을

---

41 공군 출신인 무바라크는 집권 초기 과격 보수주의자들을 퇴치하고 세력을 약화시켜 국가를 안정화하는 데 성공했다. 그러나 이 과정에서 국가비상령을 내리고 강경책을 펼쳐 국민의 자유를 박탈하며 반발을 샀다. 결국 반정부시위에 의해 2011년 2월 11일 대통령직을 사임했고 2012년 6월, 시위대 학살 혐의로 종신형을 선고받아 수감되었다.

42 하현정, 「이집트, '빵, 자유, 정의'라는 오래된 문제로의 회귀」, 『아랍의 봄 그 후 10년의 흐름』, 서울대학교출판문화원, 2022, p.42-44

바꿔 그들의 환심을 사는 일도 마다치 않았다. 그러나 자신의 독재체제에 위협으로 여겨 시종일관 적대했던 세력은 대항 부족 세력도 서구 세력도 아니었다. 그는 이슬람 극단주의 세력을 자신을 몰락시키고자 하는 타협할 수 없는 적대세력으로 규정했고, 그의 예민하고 신경질적인 반응 속에는 극단주의 세력에 대한 두려움이 감춰져 있었다.[43]

예멘의 양상을 보자. 중앙 정부는 민의적 소요에 대해 끝까지 저항하고 있다. 외교적인 술수, 권력을 이용한 탄압, 정치적 회유 등 모든 수단을 강구해 민의적 소요 앞에 누란(累卵)의 정권을 유지시키려 하고 있다. 그러나 정권 혼란을 틈타 알카에다[44]의 전략적 거점인 남부 일대를 확보하는 것에 대해서는 이상하리만치 무기력한 모습을 보이고 있다. 독재정권의 생명 연장을 위해 마지막 남은 힘을 쥐어짜느라 여력이 없는 것인지도 모른다. 혹은 정권 혼란이 가져올 극단적 체

---

43 한바란 외 7인, 「주요국의 리비아 사태에 대한 대응과 시사점」, 『오늘의 세계경제』, Vol.11 No.27, 한국대외경제정책연구원, 2011.

44 미국에서 발생한 9·11테러 배후세력으로 지목된 사우디 아라비아 출신의 오사마 빈 라덴이 조직한 이슬람주의 반미, 반유대 무장테러조직. 1980년대 소련-아프가니스탄 전쟁에 참전한 무자헤딘들을 배경으로 결성되었다. 빈 라덴 사망 후 약화되었으나 이라크 지부는 수니파 민병과 통합한 뒤, ISIS(이슬람국가)를 결성했다.

제 등장에 대해 서구에 경각심을 주려는 의도적 방관이 있을 가능성도 거론된다. 그러나 결론적으로 말하자면 이 모든 시도는 한마디로 위험천만할 뿐이다. 중동 체제에 유난히 종교, 정치, 군부 독재 정권이 많이 들어서 있어 백성들이 받는 통제와 압박은 고단하다. 그러나 대안 없는 소요의 추동은 단순한 민주화를 보장하는 것이 아니다. 서구와 중동의 역사적 경험이 다르고 프랑스 대혁명 이후 구축된 서구의 분권과 견제를 통한 민의적 통치 시스템은 오랜 세월 동안 체계적으로 축적된 역사적 체제이기 때문이다.[45]

독재를 타도하지만, 대안이 없다는 것은 종종 이슬람 극단주의자들에게 유리한 환경과 교두보를 마련한다. 이슬람 극단주의 세력의 정권화 과정에는 그들의 전략가들을 통해 사전 정권 체제의 혼란을 이용하는 전술이 주로 사용된다. 이란과 파키스탄, 수단의 경우를 보자. 그들은 정권에 대항하는 엘리트나 성난 군중들의 선동을 통해 정권의 혼란을 유도했고, 그 뒤에 통치 이념으로 이슬람 극단주의 부흥이라는 명분을 앞세워 이슬람 극단주의 통치 이념을 제시했다. 그

---

[45] 황의현, 「예멘, 겨울보다 시린 봄」, 『아랍의 봄 그 후 10년의 흐름』, 서울대학교 출판문화원, 2022, p.85-98

것은 서구에 대해 불신과 이용만 당해온 역사적 피해의식으로 서구적 통치 모델을 따르는 것에도 부담이 있으며, 독재정권의 무능과 억압으로도 돌아가고 싶지 않은 대중들과 대항하는 엘리트들에게 매력적인 대안, 통치 모델링으로 읽혔다. 무슬림이 독재와 서구통치 아래 불행했던 이유는 그 체제가 알라의 말씀인 코란을 따르지 않았기 때문이라고 말하며, 무함마드의 생전의 역사적 경험으로 돌아가 통치 체계를 만들 때 이전과 다른 통치가 임할 것이라는 설명은 무슬림들에게 거부할 수 없는 유혹이 되곤 했다. 그러나 이러한 지하디스트의 선동이 이슬람 종교, 정치 지도자들이 말하는 코란에 입각한 통치라는 말과는 사뭇 다른 제안이라는 것을 순진한 무슬림들은 언뜻 들어서는 깊이 이해하지 못한다. 양심과 민족주의에 근거한 이슬람 체계는 코란을 교리상으로 재해석해 폭력적 역사와 기능을 교묘히 수정했지만, 이슬람 극단주의자들의 코란 해석은 코란이 발생한 시기의 역사적 상황에 대한 이해 없이 문자 그대로의 코란을 받아들여 폭력 사용의 정당성을 옹호하는 방향으로 이루어진다.[46]

---

46   브리태니커 편찬위원회(2017), 앞의 책, p.236-241.

이것은 상상의 모델링이 아니다. 이란과 파키스탄, 수단의 이슬람 극단주의 세력의 집권과 유사한 정치적 발흥이 위와 같은 과정을 통해 이루어졌다. 앞으로 이슬람 극단주의 세력이 정권의 혼란을 이용하리라는 것은 당연한 접근이다. 빈 라덴이 죽기 직전에 한 성명을 통해 그의 관심인 미국을 비롯한 서구에 대한 투쟁과 더불어 중동 소요 사태로 인한 통치의 혼란을 이용해서 이슬람 극단주의 세력과 그 정권을 추동해 보려는 시도가 있었다는 것은 이미 여러 정보로부터 밝혀져 왔다.[47] 이것은 빈 라덴의 사고방식으로 볼 때 의외로운 것이다. 왜냐하면, 그에게 있어 이슬람의 부패는 서구 세력의 개입 때문이며 이슬람 극단주의 통치에 의한 칼리프 체제로 복원하기에 앞서, 먼저는 이 모든 악의 머리이자 근원인 서구 미국과 이스라엘을 제거하는 것이 그의 투쟁의 일차적 과정이었기 때문이다.[48] 투쟁노선 순서과정의 앞뒤를 바꿀 만큼 빈

---

47 NBC Nightly News, "Bin Laden Documents Revealed | NBC Nightly News", NBC News, 2015.05.22, https://www.youtube.com/watch?v=qAJDqVudfPw

48 빈라덴은 사이드쿠틉의 사상에 주로 영감을 받았으나 이슬람주의자들이 지역 정권이나 이스라엘을 전복 대상으로 삼기에 앞서 미국 공격에 먼저 집중해야 한다고 주장했다.
9/11위원회, 「미국에 대한 테러 공격에 관한 국가 위원회의 최종 보고서(The 9/11 Commission Report)」, 2004, p.54-55.

라덴이 중동 소요 사태를 이슬람 극단주의를 세력화할 적합한 방법으로 보았다는 뜻이다.

중동 독재정권에는 두려움이라는 역설이 존재한다. 그들은 종종 통치를 위해 정권 존립에 위협이 되는 세력을 만날 때 두려움을 주기 위한 공포 정치를 사용하지만, 역설적으로 독재자 자신들도 대항 세력에 대해 극단적 두려움을 가지고 있다. 또한, 이슬람 부족주의와 율법의 저변은 가문과 명예를 더럽힌 존재에 대해서는 자비가 없다.

따라서 그들의 사고는 국가체제보다 부족적 가문과 명예에 훨씬 실제적인 권위로 두고 따른다. 중동에서 어느 정도 부족과 율법적 체제를 견제하지 않고는 독재적 권력이라는 것은 존립할 수 없다. 따라서 몇몇 부족에 대한 회의와 이슬람 율법의 수용과 타협을 통해 중동 내 독재정권이 생겼다 하더라도 정권이 전복되면 상황은 달라진다. 적대적 처지에 있었던 부족과 '눈에는 눈, 이에는 이'라는 중동의 율법적 사고방식이 독재자들을 권좌에서 끌어내릴 때 극단적 처형과 원수 갚음으로 처리하게 한다.[49] 이집트의 무바라크나 리비아의 카다피, 예멘의 살레 등은 모두 이러한 몰락을 경험하거나 비슷한 길을 걸을 것이다. 절대 권력이었던 중동의 독재자들도 실상은 중동의 소요 사태로 표출되고 있는 이슬람 백성들의 끝 간 데 없는 분노를 두려워하고 있다.

4) 통치 체계의 붕괴와 기독교

지금 중동은 구질서가 붕괴하고 있다. 그들 나름의 새로운 질서도 모색될 것이다. 이슬람 종교 독재, 왕정 독재, 군부 독재, 서구적 모델링, 민의적 소요 등에 대한 상호 충돌로 이루어진 중동 소요 사태는 새로운 질서에 대한 대안을 갈망하게 할 것이다. 그러나 불행히도 중동 땅에서 해 아래 새로운 통치 모델링은 극히 찾기 어려울 전망이다. 몇몇 중동 내부의 기독교인들은 질서의 붕괴로 인한 애꿎은 화풀이 대상이 되어 핍박을 경험할 것이며 이것은 그들을 더욱 움츠러들게 할지도 모른다. 복음이 증거 되기 위해서 구질서의 관성에 대한

---

49   에이미 추아(2020), 앞의 책, p.101-110.

충돌, 핍박은 언제나 필수 불가결한 것이다. 따라서 기독교인들은 애매한 핍박의 대상이 되어 사회적 약탈, 이민이나 유민 등 극단적 희생물이 될 가능성이 있다.[50] 이미 이집트와 시리아에서는 기독교인들에 대한 이유 없는 공격이 있었다. 중동의 기독교인들은 오래도록 이슬람 체제에 적응하기 위해 복음전파에 적극적이지 못했다.

그러나 서구에 대해 오래된 반감이 있는 중동 곳곳에서는 민의적 소요를 통한 정권 전복을 민주화로 표현하는데 별로 거부감이 없다.[51] 민주화는 다분히 서구적 용어이며 상황적 해석이다. 이 정도로 중동 전체가 서구 관념에 긍정적이고 포용적인 태도를 보인 적은 극히 드물다. 더 이상 이슬람 사회에 기독교가 곧 서구체제라는 오래된 오해는 진실이 아니다. 이슬람은 외면적으로 기독교를 모태로 차용했으며, 변용된 종교체제이고 그들은 신 자체를 배제하는 서구적 합리화보다 유일신을 인정하는 기독교에 훨씬 친근감을 가질 수 있는

---

50 박현도, 「아랍의 봄과 지하디 살라피」, 『아랍의 봄 그 후 10년의 흐름』, 서울대학교출판문화원, 2022, p.239-241.

51 엄한진, 「아랍 정치에서 민주주의의 의미와 위상: 역사적 고찰」, 『민주화 물결과 지역의 민주주의』, 한국민주주의연구소, 2012, p.250-292.

경향도 있다. 새로운 질서를 갈망하는 중동에 서구가 힘으로 접근한 오해는 복음의 희생과 포기를 통해 풀어질 수 있다. 중동 소요 사태를 통한 혼란으로 발생한 난민 등에게 복음을 통한 예수님의 진정한 통치를 말할 기회인 것이다.

중동 소요 사태로 인해 중동에는 더 이상 땅의 절망적인 아담의 체계가 아닌 하늘의 복음으로 쓰이는 새로운 질서가 들어설 가능성이 있다. 어떤 기독교인은 단지 위험하다고만 할 것이고, 어떤 기독교인은 복음으로 가능하다는 믿음으로 접근할 것이다.

참고도서 및 참조정보

- 구기연 외, 『아랍의 봄 그 후 10년의 흐름』, 서울대학교출판문화원, 2022
- 김정아 외, 『아랍의 봄: 인문학과 사회의 교차적 진화』, 세창출판사, 2022
- 노암 촘스키, 송은경 역, 『중동의 평화에 중동은 없다』, 북폴리오, 2005
- 노암 촘스키·질버트 아슈카르, 강주헌 역, 『촘스키와 아슈카르 중동을 이야기하다』, 사계절, 2009
- 니얼 퍼거슨, 홍기빈 역, 『광장과 타워』, 아르테, 2019
- 데이비드 프롬킨, 이순호 역, 『현대 중동의 탄생』, 갈라파고스, 2015
- 로레타 나폴레오니, 노만수·정태영 역, 『이슬람 불사조(이슬람국가IS의 정체와 중동의 재탄생)』, 글항아리, 2015
- 램지 바루드, 최유나 역, 『이슬람 전사의 향과 투쟁』, 산수야, 2016
- 르몽드 디플로마티크 엮음, 『르몽드 인문학(세계의 석학들이 말하는 지구 공존의 법칙)』, 휴먼큐브, 2014
- 리처드 부커, 서광훈 역, 『이슬람의 거룩한 전쟁 지하드』, 스톤스프, 2013
- 마이클 S. 최, 허석재 역, 『사람들은 어떻게 광장에 모이는 것일까』, 후마니타스, 2014
- 마이클 와이스·하산 하산, 김정우·이예라·박지민 역, 『알라의 사생아IS』, 영림카디널, 2015
- 마크 A. 가브리엘, 이찬미 역, 『이슬람과 테러리즘 그 뿌리를 찾아서』, 글마당, 2009
- 마크 A. 가브리엘, 4HIM 역, 『이슬람과 유대인 그 끝나지 않은 전쟁』, 글마당, 2009
- 명지대학교 중동문제연구소 엮음, 『IS를 말한다』, 모시는사람들, 2015
- 발터 샤이델, 조미현 역, 『불평등의 역사』, 에코리브르, 2017
- 버나드 루이스, 『이슬람 1400년』, 까치, 2010
- 버나드 루이스, 이희수 역, 『중동의 역사』, 까치, 1998
- 브리태니커 편찬위원회, 『브리태니커 필수 교양사전 이슬람』, 아고라, 2017
- 사뮈엘 로랑, 은정 펠스너 역, 『IS 리포트』, 한울, 2015
- 사이드 쿠틉, 서정민 역, 『진리를 향한 이정표(이슬람 원리주의 혁명의 실천적 지침서)』, 평사리, 2011
- 송경근, 「이븐 칼둔의 아사비야에 대한 연구」, 『한국중동학회논총』 제 36권 제 3호, 2016
- 손주영, 황병하 외, 『1400년 이슬람 문명의 길을 걷다』, 프라하, 2012
- 수잔벅 모스, 윤일성·김주영 역, 『꿈의 세계와 파국 대중 유토피아의 소멸』, 경성대학교출판부, 2008
- 쉴레이만 세이디, 곽영완 역, 『터키 민족 2천년 사』, 애플미디어, 2012
- 아자 가트, 오숙은·이재만 역, 『문명과 전쟁』, 교유서가, 2017
- 아이라 M. 라피두스, 신연성 역, 『이슬람의 세계사1』, 이산, 2008
- 아이라 M. 라피두스, 신연성 역, 『이슬람의 세계사2』, 이산, 2008
- 알렉스 캘리니코스·크리스 하먼 외 3명, 『이집트 혁명과 중동의 민중 반란』, 책갈피, 2011
- 야마우치 마사유키, 이용빈 역, 『이슬람의 비극』, 한울아카데미, 2017
- 엄한진, 「아랍 정치에서 민주주의의 의미와 위상: 역사적 고찰」, 『민주화물결과 지역의 민주주의』, 한국민주주의연구소, 2012
- 앨버트 후라니, 김정명·홍미정 역, 『아랍인의 역사』, 심산, 2010

- 에이미 추아, 김승진 역, 『정치적 부족주의』, 부키, 2020
- 엘리아스 카네티, 강두식·박병덕 역, 『군중과 권력』, 바다출판사, 2010
- 요제프 보단스키, 최인자 역, 『오사마 빈 라덴』, 명상, 2001
- 요코타 다카유키 외, 이용빈 역, 『아랍의 심장에서는 무슨 일이 벌어지고 있는가』, 한울아카데미, 2016
- 윌리엄 와그너, 노승현 역, 『이슬람의 세계 변화 전략』, APOSTOLOSPRESS, 2007
- 유진 로건, 이은정 역, 『아랍(오스만 제국에서 아랍 혁명까지)』, 까치, 2022
- 이븐할둔, 김호동 역, 『역사서설』, 까치, 2003
- 이지은(세계지역연구센터 아프리카중동팀 전문연구원),
  「베냐민 네타냐후 총리 재집권 이후 이스라엘의 정세 변화와 시사점」, 『KIEP 세계경제 포커스』,
  Vol.6 No 6, KIEP 대외경제정책연구원, 2023
- 전완경, 『아랍문화사』, 한국학술정보, 2013
- 제인 비뱅크, 프레더릭 쿠퍼, 이재만 역, 『세계제국사』, 책과함께, 2016
- 존 던, 강철웅·문지영 역, 『민주주의 수수께끼』, 후마니타스, 2015
- 최영길, 『아랍에서 출발한 이슬람의 역사와 문화』, 세창출판사, 2014
- 칼라 파워, 하윤숙 역, 『문명의 만남(세상의 절반, 이슬람을 알기 위해 떠나는 여행)』, 세종서적, 2019
- 캐스 R. 선스타인, 이정인 역, 『우리는 왜 극단에 끌리는가』, 프리뷰, 2011
- 타마라 손, 김문주 역, 『어떻게 이슬람은 서구의 적이 되었는가(이슬람에 대한 서구의 오해와 편견)』,
  시그마북스, 2017
- 타밈 안사리, 류한원 역, 『이슬람의 눈으로 본 세계사』, 뿌리와이파리, 2011
- 파스칼 보니파스, 최린 역, 『지정학: 지금 세계에 무슨 일이 벌어지고 있는가』, 가디언, 2019
- 피터 자이한, 홍지수 역, 『각자도생의 세계와 지정학』, 김앤김북스, 2021
- 피터 자이한, 홍지수 역, 『붕괴하는 세계와 인구학』, 김앤김북스, 2023
- 하메드 압드엘-사마드, 배명자 역, 『무함마드 평전(선지자에서 인간으로)』, 한스미디어, 2016
- 하영식, 『분쟁전문기자 하영식 IS를 말하다』, 불어라바람아, 2015
- 한국이슬람학회, 『세계의 이슬람』, 청아출판사, 2018
- 한바란 외 7인, 「주요국의 리비아 사태에 대한 대응과 시사점」, 『오늘의 세계경제』, Vol.11 No.27,
  한국대외경제정책연구원, 2011
- 한스 큉, 『한스 큉의 이슬람』, 시와진실, 2012
- 9/11위원회, 『미국에 대한 테러 공격에 관한 국가 위원회의 최종 보고서(The 9/11 Commission Report)』, 2004

참고도서 및 참조정보

· ACLED, "Increasing tribal resistance to Houthi rule", reliefweb, 2019.03.07, https://reliefweb.int/report/yemen/increasing-tribal-resistance-houthi-rule
· Ali Abunimah, "Hamas Election Victory: A Vote for Clarity", The Electronic Intifada, 2006.01.26, https://electronicintifada.net/content/hamas-election-victory-vote-clarity/5847
· ALJAZEERA AND NEWS AGENCIES, "Israeli settlers set up new illegal outpost on Palestinian land", ALJAZEERA, 2023.06.22, https://www.aljazeera.com/news/2023/6/22/israeli-settlers-set-up-new-illegal-outpost-on-palestinian-land
· Africanews with United Nations, "Muammar Gaddafi at the 64th UN General Assembly in 2009", Africanews, 2019.09.12., https://www.africanews.com/2017/09/19/speech-muammar-gaddafi-at-the-64th-un-general-assembly-in-2009/ · BBC NEWS, "Israel backs new Jewish settlement homes", 2013.08.11, https://www.bbc.com/news/world-middle-east-23655661
· BBC News, "1970: Civil war breaks out in Jordan", http://news.bbc.co.uk/onthisday/hi/dates/stories/september/17/newsid_4575000/4575159.stm
· BBC News Korea, "What is the Rafa Checkpoint, which is a 'lifeline to Gaza'?", 2023.11.02, https://www.bbc.com/korean/articles/ce9l8jnd613o
· BBC News Korea, "Who is the Lebanese armed group Hezbollah?", 2023.10.18., https://www.bbc.com/korean/articles/cd1qgmq4z15o
· Dario Sabaghi, "Are Hezbollah and Israel edging closer to war?", THE NEW ARAB, 2024.01.15, https://www.newarab.com/analysis/are-hezbollah-and-israel-edging-closer-war
· Kali Robinson, Council on Foreign Relations, "What is Hezbollah? What to know about its origins, structure and history", PBS NEWS HOUR, 2023.10.16., https://www.pbs.org/newshour/world/what-is-hezbollah-what-to-know-about-its-origins-structure-and-history
· Laila Bassam and Maya Gebeily, "Israeli strike kills a Hezbollah commander in Lebanon", REUTERS, 2024.01.09, https://www.reuters.com/world/middle-east/israeli-strike-lebanon-kills-senior-commander-elite-hezbollah-unit-security-2024-01-08/
· Martin Chulov, The Guardian, 2014.07.06, "Abu Bakr al-Baghdadi emerges from shadows to rally Islamist followers", https://www.theguardian.com/world/2014/jul/06/abu-bakr-al-baghdadi-isis
· Mustafa Fetouri, "Libya's human rights situation is worse than what it was under Gaddafi", MIDDLE EAST MONITOR, 2023.04.13, https://www.middleeastmonitor.com/20230413-libyas-human-rights-situation-is-worse-than-what-it-was-under-gaddafi/
· NBC Nightly News, "Bin Laden Documents Revealed | NBC Nightly News", NBC News, 2015.05.22, https://www.youtube.com/watch?v=qAJDqVudfPw
· Pierre Tristam, "Black September: The Jordanian-PLO Civil War of 1970", ThoughtCo., 2019.07.03,

https://www.thoughtco.com/black-september-jordanian-plo-civil-war-2353168
· Simon Tisdall, "The collapse of Isis will inflame the regional power struggle", The Guardian, 2019.02.17, https://www.theguardian.com/world/2019/feb/17/isis-rout-inflames-regional-power-struggle
· Yolande Knell, BBC News, "West Bank: US 'troubled' by Israeli settlement expansion plans", 2023.06.27, https://www.bbc.com/news/world-middle-east-66027025

Contents

Preface — 105

Thanks to — 111

I A Study on the trends and flows of Islamic extremism in the Middle East viewed from the Israel-Hamas war — 113
   - Possibilities and prospects of Palestinian refugee missions in Arab countries

1 Overview — 115

2 Hamas, a discrete organization network and a complex of system transplantation. The trend of extreme organization with hybrid mixing aspects and its origin. — 123

3 Aliyah Movement, Jewish Zionism and Christianity, and the issue of establishing Jewish settlements in Palestine — 142

4 The possibility of refugee accommodation and refugee - oriented missions in countries adjacent to Israel and Palestine (Egypt, Jordan, and Lebanon) from a historical perspective. — 148

5 Conclusion & Forecast — 159

II The origins and research tasks of the Arab - the remaining nation, Timely situational analysis
- Focusing on Arab tribalism

167

1 **Raising Questions about the Origins of Arabs**   169
 - Pondering the roots of Arab tribalism

2 **Beyond Research Constraints**   172
 - The absence of records of Arab nomadic culture and the Utilization of Islamic Intellectual Archives Injected with Hellenic Intellect

3 **The Origins of Arabs in the Bible** - The Arab lineage traces back to Ishmael and Muhammad   174

4 **Research on Arab origins and redefinition of research categories for introductory Arabic studies, Middle Eastern studies, and Islamic studies** - Including the North Africa region, Central Asia region, and Southeast Asia region   177

5 **Arab Root Tribalism, Muhammad, and Israel Hamas War and Peace Solutions**   182

6 **Examining the Arab Spring through the Lens of Arab Islamic Tribalism**   187

Reference books and information   218

Notice

This article was written around January 2024.

I would like to inform you that the introduction has started to be written in the form of a column for the column contribution to 『Korean Journal of Frontier Missions』.

Preface

Spaces and times are intertwined in the center of the world. The spiritualities of the ancient and medieval periods have been revived, and the number of overlapping aspects in the hypermodern era has increased significantly. Phenomena that were once geographically distinct are strangely crossing and intertwining. Therefore, events that are difficult to interpret with previous perspectives are rapidly occurring and accumulating, leading toward a new era.

The ancient and medieval concepts of Islam have accumulated like moss, and the zeitgeist of the Arab Middle East is still manifesting and repeatedly applied as a phenomenon that is a variation of that era. Similarly, Islamic extremism is a phenomenon that draws its motives from the personality of Muhammad and the Caliphate era. However, it is clear that Hamas, which can be considered a disciple of Muhammad, Hassan al-Banna, and Sayyid Qutb, is using the cryptocurrency Bitcoin as war funds or to maintain his regime. This is a new phenomenon that occurred in the era of the Fourth Industrial Revolution, which did not exist in ancient or medieval times.

ISIS Khorasan(ISIS-K) carried out a theater terror attack in the heart of a Russian city while Russia is at war in Ukraine. While there are scholars' opinions on whether Russia's confrontation with the West by stimulating the affinity between North Korea and China in the former Soviet Union in front of NATO's consolidation will revive the new Cold War era, Islamic extremists have entered Russia, the axis of the new Cold War confrontation, and carried out a bomb attack. Putin immediately acknowledged that this was the work of ISIS but claimed that Ukraine was behind it. Is it possible to interpret this situation only within the framework of the modern Cold War or through the analytical framework of Islamic extremism, which is an extreme layering of religious spirituality in ancient Islam?

Moreover, the fact that artificial intelligence (AI) has already executed the decision-making authority to kill humans in the war between Ukraine and Russia. Isn't it a sign of how quickly the times and eras are changing? In this era of rapid change, where artificial intelligence programs are already capable of killing people and making decisions about life and death, how can we diagnose this phenomenon biblically and interpret it in advance like a prophet?

This book is a small research result in an era where new phenomena and timely information are overflowing, and interdisciplinary research and traditional academic research are struggling to keep up with the increasingly frequent occurrence of phenomena such as the mixing of time and space in the world. Traditional scholarship has a framework for verifying human cognitive errors based on inductive research. Moreover, interdisciplinary research attempts to respond to phenomena where time and space are intertwined by synthesizing multiple disciplinary perspectives into two or more.

However, verifying errors in the renewal and generation of human intellectual claims requires a significant amount of time for objective evidence for generalization, cross-validation, and paradigm formation based on the form of papers. While hypermodern phenomena are rapidly occurring, accumulating, and overflowing with timely IT information, the weakness of traditional scholarship lies in its overly slow verification process and speed.

The Israel-Hamas war became known to the world through IT information, SNS, and real-time videos rather than through traditional academic paper information. Scholars are increasingly interpreting situations and phenomena based on IT information and immediately expressing their opinions rather than entering that world to study and refine their arguments through academic research because the phenomena are spreading too quickly and having a massive impact on the world.

However, while such IT information allows for quick information gathering, it has a fatal weakness in that it is difficult to filter out biased errors in human cognitive information recognition, such as confirmation bias, without verification by traditional scholarship. Therefore, the world now needs eyes that can stand between traditional scholarship and IT information and provide quick and relatively accurate intellectual interpretation.

Crucially, the human history from ancient times to the present day must be interpreted in light of the truth of the Bible. Arabs, who gave rise to Islam, are descendants of Ishmael in the Bible, and the Bible has already interpreted his life and worldview.

In addition, while artificial intelligence and bitcoin are new technological phenomena that belong to the 4th Industrial Revolution, the Bible has already interpreted the human nature that developed asphalt-like bitumen, a new technology at that time, in the story of the Tower of Babel.

Therefore, in a world where time and space are intertwined and eras change rapidly, people of truth who interpret the world from a biblical perspective are more important than ever amid the flood of interdisciplinary research and IT information. I hope this little piece will be a small motif or material for such people.

End of March. 2024
Amidst the news of AI killing in the Russia-Ukraine war,
Amidst the dark clouds of declarations of war from Israel, Hezbollah, and Iran,
With a heart that clings to the unshakable truth as a signpost,

Missionary David Cho

Thanks to

Thanks for all advanced of faith who was being inspiration of nourish- ment and also I thank you all staff Kyoungeun Yu, Hyeji Park who helped proofreading and editing, and staff Hyeog-gi Gwon who did graceful design, and staff Siwon Park, Haeun Ban, Hee Myeong Kim who did translation, and about 350 mission staffs who works together in Vision Mission community.

My family a wife and Eunbit, Sihoo and Annyeong are my treasures who never reject the community lifestyle to live with the word of God. Of course the Lord will pick up the torch of His word to light dark age beside us, but that is why I am really appreciate His word is with us.

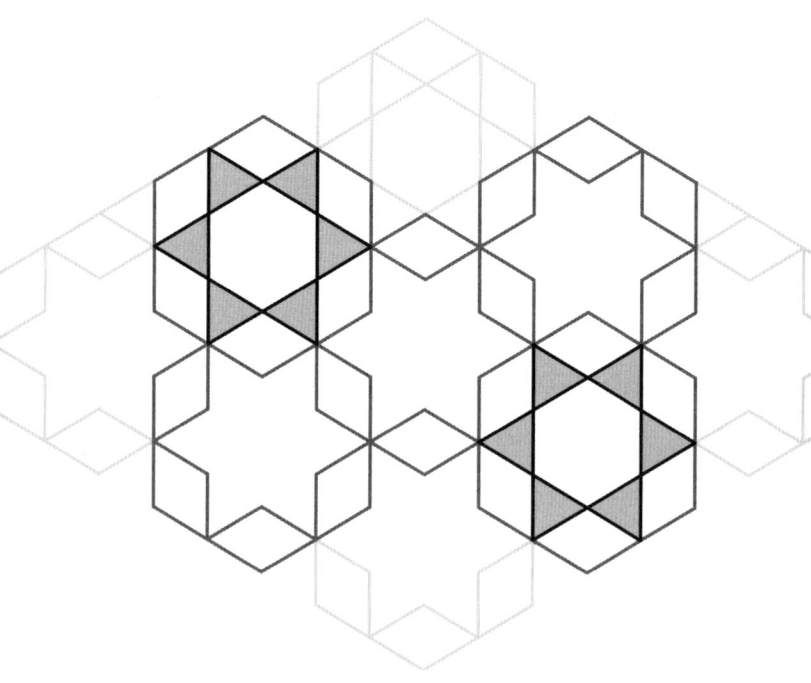

I

A Study on the trends and flows of Islamic extremism in the Middle East viewed from the Israel–Hamas war

- Possibilities and prospects of Palestinian refugee missions in Arab countries

1 Overview

With the end of the Cold War era around 2000, the axis of global conflict in the world shifted to the confrontation between Islamic terrorism and the West through the 9/11 incident.[1] Osama bin Laden and Al-Qaeda[2] who drove the 9/11 incident, were not from an Islamic extremism discrete organization network movement that suddenly emerged. They have long been activists who were influenced by the Islamic extremism ideology of 'Sayyid Qutb[3]'(the second leader of the

---

[1] A simultaneous multiple suicide aircraft terrorist attack on the 110-story World Trade Center(WTC) twin buildings in New York, USA and the Pentagon building in Washington on September 11, 2001. This incident resulted in nearly 3,000 deaths.

[2] A Sunni extremist terrorist group organized by Osama Bin Laden, they are identified as the force behind the 9/11 terrorist attacks in the US.

[3] He is a proponent of the 'Islamic ideologizing' and 'Islamic revolution' that presented a new milestone for the Islamic extremism movement by refining and systematizing Islamic extremism theory and behavioral philosophy. He is considered one of the most influential figures in the Islamic extremism movement that is taking place throughout Egypt and the Muslim world today.

Muslim Brothers[4]), which is an armed struggle in a violent line against the West. Through the Taliban war in Afghanistan, the United States aimed to destroy the network of Islamic terrorism discrete organizations such as Al-Qaeda. However, after the Iraq war, ISIS[5] emerged by taking advantage of the chaos of the war, rather than achieving the annihilation of the Islamic extremism discrete organization network that had spread across world borders. Thus, attempts to transplant the Islamic extremism system were rampant, giving rise to the transplanting stage of the extremism system in Syria and Iraq which claimed to be an Islamic state during the Caliphate era. It was an attempt

---

4 The world's largest and best Islamic organization with an estimated 5~10 million members. It is an Islamic fundamentalism organization founded in 1928 by an Egyptian Islamic scholar and social activist Hasan al-banna in Ismailia, Suez, with the goal of 'implementing and spreading true Islamic values'.

5 The Islamic State of Iraq and Syria(ISIS) is a radical Sunni militant group, also known as the Islamic State of Iraq and the Levant(ISIL). Started as a sub-organization of al-Qaeda in Iraq in 2003. Rapidly expanded its power and changed its name to the Islamic State(IS) in 2014 by promoting Abu Bakr al-Baghdadi as caliph. Then expanded its power mainly in Iraq and Syria. It collapsed respectively with the loss of Mosul(Iraq) and its capital Raqqa(Syria), in July and October 2017. Later, Baghouz(last base) was lost to the Syrian Democratic Forces(SDF) in March 2019.

to transplant a more malicious Islamic extremism system by emerged ISIS, compared to the Islamic extremism discrete organization movement period represented by Al-Qaeda immediately after 9/11.

As is well known, in Oct. 2023, the armed faction terrorist organization Hamas[6] in Palestine triggered a series of cruel incidents, kidnapped and killed Jewish civilians and detained as prisoners of war, leading to a war between Hamas and Israel. Prime Minister Benjamin Netanyahu's cabinet and the Israeli government were already strongly inclined to fundamentalism

---

6 A representative armed group in Palestine who is leading terrorism against Israel, it constitutes the two major political factions along with Fatah in Palestine. After winning the 2006 Palestinian general election, it ousted Fatah from the Gaza Strip in 2007 and rueled the Gaza Strip independently.

based on Zionism[7]. It was also a time when issues such as illegal Jewish settlements[8] were causing violent conflict between Palestinians and Jews in the West Bank[9].

Against this background, what kind of organization is Hamas that caused a war that could be considered a national

---

7 Prime Minister Netanyahu returned to power in Nov. 2022. This government came to power based on the success of uniting far-right groups and is evaluated as having the most far-right tendency in Israeli history. The situation in Israel was becoming unstable due to strong policies against Palestine and judicial reform.
Ji Eun Lee, 「Changes in the situation in Israel and implications after Prime Minister Benjamin Netanyahu's return to power」, 『KIEP World Economic Focus』, Vol.6 No 6, Korea Institute for International Economic Policy, 2023

8 It refers to the Jewish residential area in the Gaza Strip and the West Bank which is Palestine autonomous region. The international community has declared it illegal to build Jewish settlements in the West Bank(Israel occupied during the Third Middle East War in 1967) and is demanding an end to it. (International Court of Justice & U.N. Security Council)

9 Antonio Guterres(UN Setretary-General) said, "Settlement construction in the West Bank is causing tension and violence, hindering the establishment of permanent peace." and called for an immediate halt to all activities related to settlement in Israel.
AL JAZEERA AND NEWS AGENCIES, "Israeli settlers set up new illegal outpost on Palestinian land", ALJAZEERA, 2023.06.22.

war between countries? Are they a terrorist organization like a discrete organization Al-Qaeda which is provoking asymmetric warfare?[10] They are also a cross-border discrete organization network in that they have branches not only in Israel but also in Qatar and Turkey. Also, are they a governance system like a country that takes over the power? Of course they are also the political faction that has taken power in Palestine through elections since 2006[11]. They are a hybrid form of discrete organization and governance system that simultaneously combined aspects of terrorism in the form of Al-Qaeda as a discrete organization network, which has emerged sequentially in the wake of Islamic extremism trends since the 2000s, and aspects of ISIS as an extremism system that had established a

---

10 It is a type of war between belligerent groups that have significantly different military capabilities, strategies, or tactics. It refers to a conflict in which the enemy is not the country's regular army, and includes rebels, resistance movements, guerrilla warfare, counterinsurgency warfare, terrorism, and counter-terrorism activities.

11 On Jan. 25, 2006, Hamas won the general election for the Legislative Council of Palestinian Authority, winning 44.45%, 74 out of 132 seats.
Ali Abunimah, "Hamas Election Victory: A Vote for Clarity", The Electronic Intifada, 2006.01.26.

governance system.

According to recent Islamic terrorism trends, it is necessary to look at the reason why Hamas was launched as a Palestinian branch of the Egyptian Muslim Brotherhood rather than being influenced solely by Al-Qaeda or ISIS.[12] Therefore, it seems that its motif and origin should be found in the ancestor of the Muslim Brotherhood, while it was a political faction inherent in the origins of the emergence, which later added armed struggle and took the terrorism line. Thus, I would like to explain the background of the Muslim Brotherhood founder 'Hassan Al Banna[13]', who made it possible to create about 500 branches, as a public teacher, and the subsequent approach to the faction political system of the Islamic fundamentalism movement. Then, by explaining the background of the second leader Sayyid Qutb,

---

[12] Hamas was officially recognized as a branch of the Muslim Brotherhood until the announcement amendments to the Article 42 Charter 2017. Dr. Hyun Do Park(Sogang Uni, Euro-MENA Institute), 2023. https://youtu.be/FW0XOfgoiYk?si=s29eMR9k0qNj2vil

[13] Ju Young Son, Byung Ha Hwang, etc. 「Walking the path of Islamic Civilization in 1400 years」, Prague, 2012, p736.

adding the line of armed struggle to the Muslim Brotherhood, I would like to describe how his thoughts influenced the terrorism of the line of armed struggle activated to the discrete organization network. In addition, if space allows, I would like to look at the frontline confronting Israel in the north and point out the tendency of the mixed system and discrete organization and emerging aspects of the Shia extremism political faction Hezbollah(It was founded with receiving name and statements from Ayatollah Ruhollah Khomeini(Iran) when he established theocratic fundamentalism Islamic regime in Iran).[14]

Additionally, the issue of Jewish illegal settlements is related to the return of diaspora Jews and the influx of converted Jews from abroad, who carried out the Aliyah movement religiously through Israel's right-wing shift and fundamentalist

---

[14] "The state system presented by Khomeini is the 'Islamic jurist governance system', which is a hybrid form of theocracy and republican government. Nam Sik In(Professor in Korea National Diplomatic Academy & director of Middle East research team), 2022. https://youtu.be/0dv_vZR1oLQ?si=m4flMeZUZfWhdmiz

Zionism. There is a trend of supporting this movement[15] in some Christianity, so I would like to explain how this influence has aggravated the issue of illegal settlements, not only from a religious ideology but also from the perspective of international regional studies. At the end of this article, while pointing out the latest issues in the field under the line of fundamentalism and extremism that are having a huge impact and influence in the Middle East, I also look into the possibility of accepting refugees arising during the war in neighboring countries(Jordan, Egypt, and Lebanon) against a historical background. Then I would like to explore the accessibility of the Palestinian refugee ministry.

---

15 A movement in which the Jewish diaspora scattered around the world returned to the Jewish land of Israel. The Law of Return, passed by the Israeli parliament in 1950, grants all Diaspora Jews and their children and grandchildren the right to immigrate to Israel and obtain Israeli citizenship based on their connection to Jewish identity.

2 Hamas, a discrete organization network and a complex of system transplantation.
The trend of extreme organization with hybrid mixing aspects and its origin.

Now, Hamas is waging war on behalf of their country against Israel, a military power. It has both aspects of a discrete network and a system simultaneously. Hamas has a hybrid tendency of mixing between the discrete network movement (which derived from the Islamic fundamentalism organization Al-Qaeda, which emerged after the 2000s) and ISIS, which attempted system transplanting. Al-Qaeda gave the powerhouse, the United States, a hard time by provoking asymmetrical warfare when the distinction between civil society and the front line was unclear.[16] Also, ISIS self-actualized the implantation of the caliphate system in the Middle East and brought chaos for a while, which became an international challenge.[17] Extremism networks and systems emerged through gradual waves in the 2000s and 2010s, showing what kind of global problems and harmful effects they can demonstrate historically and periodically.

Hamas is a relatively small organization compared to the previous two organizations, Al-Qaeda and ISIS. However, if Hamas operates in the Middle East as a hybridism organization that effectively demonstrates the network and system aspects of these two organizations (or if another similar Islamic

---

16 Bin Laden established a large-scale organization in Sudan that combined business and terrorism. An Al-Qaeda member traveled from Western Europe to the Far East as the CEO of Bin Laden's investment company, organizing business companies and non-governmental organizations. At the same time, those offices were used to support financial and other needs of terrorist activities. 9/11Commission, 「Final Report on Terrorist Attacks Upon the Unite States(The 9/11 Commission Report)」, 2004, p.57.

17 Amy Chua, Translated by Seung Jin Kim, 「Political Tribes: Group Instinct and the Fate of Nation」, Bookie, 2020, p.137-143.

extremism organization emerges in a hybrid form), it can even cause more harm to the world and the Middle East compared to Al-Qaeda or ISIS. Therefore, we must closely watch it based on the mission perspective.

Anyhow, these aspects of Hamas as a network of discrete organizations, a governmental ruling system, and their structural systems were influenced by the following factors. Either they were influenced by existing Islamic extremist philosophers and activists (Hassan al-Banna, Qutb, Osama bin Laden, etc.) or were mutually influenced by fundamentalist and extremist organizations (Muslim Brotherhood, Al-Qaeda, and ISIS), depending on their ramifications in each era. Therefore, let's take a look at the extremist philosophers, activists, and organizations that inspired these two aspects and deeply influenced the organization so-called Hamas(which started as a Palestinian branch of the Muslim Brotherhood and now exists as a Palestinian government system, with discrete organizations in Turkey, Qatar, [18]etc.). This is how we will discover that Hamas is a system but also has a network of discrete organizations at the same time, as well as the source of the recent trend of Islamic extremism that stood out through these two aspects.

1) Hassan al-Banna, founder of the Muslim Brotherhood

-Establishment of over 500 discrete organizations and political systematization due to jihad[19] against Israel.

---

18 "Hamas's Politburo members decide on fundraising and foreign policy. They are currently being provided with safe housing in Qatar." Il Gwang Sung(Korea Uni. Middle East Islam Center professor), 2023. https://youtu.be/syyO6bQNfF0?si=ArG0yqZSArZp7Jju

19 The duty achievement of jihad is divided into four categories: by the mind, by the pen, by domination, and by the sword. However, the reason why jihad has an image of violence and incitement is because radical armed organizations used to incite the public for their terrorist activities. The West also used Islam as a political tool as a challenge to their civilized society.

Hamas was founded by Sheik Ahmed Yassin[20], who studied abroad in Egypt and began as the Palestinian branch of the Muslim Brotherhood. Therefore, it can be said that Hamas was greatly influenced by the establishment process and ideology of the Egyptian Muslim Brotherhood. Hassan al-Banna, the founder of the Muslim Brotherhood, was a teacher and a member of the public service employee in the government system. Back then, the defeat of the Ottoman Caliphate to the West and the decline of the influence of Ottoman rule and subordination in Egypt was quite a historical shock to Muslims, who regarded the Ottoman Caliphate itself as a bastion of Islam.[21] In the midst of shock among Muslims, Hassan al-Banna felt that a new pivot for the Islamic spirit was needed. He founded the Muslim Brotherhood in 1928 at the age of 22, and the Muslim Brotherhood infiltrated society as a religious and political movement. It soon had a ripple effect, with over 500

---

[20] A refugee from the Gaza Strip in Palestine, he studied in Egypt and participated in the Intifada. And later founded Hamas to attack Israel, began an armed struggle, and carried out mass organization projects through religious books, sermons, and speeches.

[21] Ju Young Son, Byung Ha Hwang, etc. (2012), the book in front, p.739.

branches being created throughout Muslim society as a discrete organization and movement. Hassan al-Banna founded the Muslim Brotherhood with the goal of restoring the Islamic Caliphate system[22] in Egypt and Muslim society. This soon became oriented towards political faction and politicization, in the sense that the discrete organization movement pursued the goal of actualizing the Caliphate system. Also, as the number of Israelis immigrating to Palestine increased in 1933, Hassan al-Banna appealed the need to wage jihad against them. For this reason, the Muslim Brotherhood actually became a political organization in 1939 and was gradually rearranged.[23]

---

[22] In Arabic, it is originally 'Khalīfat rasul Allah,' and its dictionary meaning is 'representative of God's Messenger.' Caliph refers to the supreme ruler of the Islamic Empire, succeeding the Prophet Muhammad, who maintains the purity and simplicity of Islamic doctrine, protects the religion, and at the same time oversees all matters governing the Islamic community.

[23] Ju Young Son, Byung Ha Hwang, etc. (2012), the book in front, p.745-747.

2) Sayyid Qutb, the second leader of the Muslim Brotherhood
- Modern Islamic extremism philosopher who opened the introduction for adopting the armed radical struggle line and terrorism

After the founder, Hassan al-Banna, politically organized the anti-Israel resistance movement, Qutb became the second leader of the Muslim Brotherhood and gradually led the organization to a radical line.

This originated from Qutb's personal experience of isolation from the West. Sayyid Qutb, born in Egypt, went to the United States to study. With his brightness and sharp intelligence, Qutb felt severely isolated and lonely by the individualistic behavior of Westerners during his studies in the United States, and his pride was hurt. Soon, Qutb analyzed the weaknesses of Western society based on his experience.[24] He also goes on to define the corruption of Western Christian groups as the source of evil in the world order.[25] From the perspective of a Middle Easterner Qutb from the holy Islamic civilization, there seemed to be no historical justification for the holy Muslims (who strive to keep the commands of the sacred Allah and follow every jot and tittle of the law) to be dominated or to hand over the leadership to the corrupt Western civilization.

In other words, the West that Qutb experienced was corrupted by materialism, sex, momentary pleasure, and entertainment. And the West, which dominates the holy Islamic Middle Eastern civilization and insults Muslims, was nothing more than a leading power without legitimacy. Western civilization (which secured complete leadership

---

[24] Ju Young Son, Byung Ha Hwang, etc. (2012), the book in front, p.749-752.

[25] 'There is the pressure of the current difficult environment from the Western Christian world and vicious Orientalist attacks on jihad', 'Almighty Allah speaks only the truth. All the fraudsters in the Christian world who distort history are liars'
Sayyid Qutb, Translated by Jung Min Seo 『Milesstone』, Pyung Sa Li, 2011, p.184, 337.

over the Middle Eastern civilization after World War One and Two) has employed Middle Eastern Muslims who keep the holy laws as servants, gardeners, and butlers. However, the lifestyle of Westerners shown to Muslims was nothing more than a corrupted aspect of being addicted to entertainment and drugs, indulging in sex and momentary pleasure, and using materialism to control one's personality freely.

Qutb expanded the Islamic concept of jihad and actively utilized it as a struggle rather than simply as an Islamic regime. He eventually declared expulsion and resistance towards the corrupt world of Western civilization, the source of evil contaminating Islam.[26] This way, Qutb globalized the concept of jihad, which was limited to the Islamic region. Also, his idea of struggle soon provided the ideological basis for terrorism

---

26 Sayyid Qutb(2011), The book in front, p.148-153.

and the use of force.[27] Egypt's Muslim Brotherhood, which was founded under the strong influence of Qutb, has been the actual, spiritual maternity of most existing Islamic extremism terrorist groups (although it has now shifted from an armed struggling hard line to a more moderate line).

This ideology was soon implanted in Osama bin Laden and others, causing the 9/11 incident through the discrete network Al Qaeda. Therefore, it had a massive influence in encouraging the international line of struggle against the West and the global jihadist discrete organization movement.

---

[27] Omar Abdel Rahman, an extremist Islamic Imam, moved from Egypt to the United States in 1990 and preached on the content of Sayyid Qutb's 'Milesstone.' He defined the U.S. as an oppressive country of Muslims in the world and argued that it is our duty to fight against the 'enemy of God.'
9/11Commission(2004), The report in front, p.72.

3] Osama Bin Laden and Al-Qaeda
- Islamic extremism activist, who made practical transition from local jihad to global jihad and ultimately operated global discrete network movement through al-Qaeda

Osama bin Laden (who caused the 9/11 incident) is an activist who changed the direction of jihad, which had been limited to Islamic areas, to global jihad. It is a well-known fact that he is a symbolic figure of the modern Islamic extremist movement in this sense.[28] Bin Laden, who was implanted by Qutb's ideas, made it clear that the system that corrupted and polluted Islam was the United States and other Western

---

[28] When Bin Laden declared war in Feb. 1998, he had a substantial, global military organization under his command that he had been recruiting and training for over a decade. He urged other extremists to focus on attacking the U.S., saying that he did not believe it is enough to target the local government or Israel. At the same time, he claimed that he was the new movement of the future.
9/11Commission(2004), The report in front. p.54-55.

systems. He also believed that it was difficult to recreate the original version of Islam from the time of Muhammad (which was pursued by extremists) by the local jihadist movements. Bin Laden sought not to pursue religious and regional jihad but to permanently expel the Western regime that had polluted and dominated the Islamic system. So he declared and put into practice 'attacking the mainland of the United States, the head of evil.' as the jihadists[29] put it.[30]

Therefore, Osama Bin Laden should be seen as the person who led Qutb's Islamic extremism and jihadist ideological system into a full-fledged global movement or discrete organization network operation period. He is a person who changed the local jihad movement, which had remained in Islamic areas, into a global jihad movement through the 9/11 incident. For religious imams, the concept of jihad was just

---

[29] The following passages from scripture serve as motivation for jihadists to fight: "Permission to fight back is hereby granted to those being fought, for they have been wronged. And Allah is truly Most Capable of helping them prevail."(Quran 22:39)

[30] Amy Chua(2020), the book in front, p.145.

religious laws that Muslims must obey at the will of Allah, and for modern extreme jihadists, it was just a local armed struggle within the Islamic region or at its borders. However, Osama bin Laden is the person who drove the international movement that transformed the extremism movement of jihadists into a global jihad rather than simply an Islamic regional boundary. He became an international leader and symbolic icon of global jihad.[31] He also linked Al-Qaeda's cross-border discrete organizations against the United States (which they had identified as their main enemy) and the West. Therefore, he showed his ability to deal with powerful countries with minimal power through asymmetric warfare rather than in the form of nation-to-state warfare.

---

31 A document has been released that contains Osama Bin Laden's strategy and instructions urging Al-Qaeda and its overseas followers to focus attacks on the U.S. and the West before forming an Islamic State.
NBC News, 2015.05.22., "Bin Laden Documents Revealed | NBC Nightly News"

4) ISIS as regime transplant
- Restoration of the Islamic Caliphate and attempts to implant an extremism system

In ISIS, which claims to restore the Islamic Caliphate system, no heroic figures or names are highlighted. This is because ISIS dreams of transplanting a system beyond the activities of activists and crusaders. Naturally, more emphasis is placed on the system of the Islamic state rather than on the person. Only the Islamic expansion history of Muhammad and his successor, the Caliphate, is the uncontaminated form of Islam recognized by Islamic extremists.[32] It is believed that the demise of the Caliphate system and the ruling of the Islamic dynasty system

---

32 The early Muslims were able to remain a special generation, distinct from other generations in history, because they drank from one spring water. But over time, other sources and teachings began to mix with this spring water. Later Muslims polluted pure Islam by accepting Greek philosophy and logic, ancient Persia tales and ideas, Jewish scriptures and traditions, Christian theology, and even the dregs of other religions and civilizations.
Sayyid Qutb(2011), the book in front, p68-69.

in the form of bloodline hereditary succession is no longer the original form of Islam.

Therefore, jihadists, including ISIS, believe that only the recovery and restoration of the Islamic Caliphate system (the prototype of the Islamic system) can be the answer to the world. According to jihadists, the ecumenical Islamic empire, as the prototype of Islamic rule expressed by Allah through Muhammad and the caliphs, was not a bloodline hereditary system. The prototype of the Islamic system was the caliphate system, in which power was transferred to a leadership system based on spiritual leadership. Jihadists believe that the Koran and Sunnah[33], or Allah's Sharia law, acknowledge only this original caliphate. They even reject not only the Western system but also Islamic countries with bloodline and hereditary dynasties, considering them to be modified systems. Therefore,

---

[33] It means 'practice' in Arabic. After Islam was founded by Muhammad, the meaning of the Sunnah changed, and it came to point to things that Muslims should take as an example, such as Muhammad's words and actions.

restoring this caliphate system commanded by Allah's Sharia law is the only way to correct the corruption and pollution of the world that does not obey Allah's law.[34]

Therefore, the goal of extremists is not simply to build a discrete network of jihadists while driving an Islamic extremism movement around the world through global jihad. They want to actualize their dream of restoring the Caliphate based on this network. Jihadists believe that the Caliphate is the only system on earth commanded by the law of Allah. For them, the caliphate system is a struggling utopian goal to simultaneously eliminate and transform the Middle Eastern system contaminated by Western liberalism, nationalism,

---

[34] "We must return to the purest source from which the early Muslims received their teachings. That is, the purest source that was not adulterated or contaminated with anything else. And from that pure source, we must establish standards and find answers in all areas, including our lives, the foundation of the government system, politics, and the economy."
Sayyid Qutb(2011), the book in front, p75.

socialism, and dynastic systems.[35]

In addition, as Muhammad and the Caliph demonstrated, the Caliphate system was expanded through war, so the tactical strategies utilized by Muhammad and the Caliph around the 7th century were fully justified. It provides legitimacy, as shown by the early Islamic system, which occurred in wartime situations that were used as a means of Islamic expansion not only during the advance war but also during the Caliphate period, since the 'Hegira[36]' (Muhammad's migration from Mecca). It includes capture, lies and propaganda tactics, reversal

---

[35] "As a result, no group of people with the same capabilities as the early Muslims appears in the present era. Therefore, in order to advance the Islamic movement and begin training and education for it, it is absolutely necessary to separate ourselves from the influence and remnants of Jahiliyyah that is currently prevalent around us." Qutb considered present Islamic countries as Jahiliyyah and made them targets of extreme Islamism struggle.

[36] On Sep. 25th, 622, Prophet Muhammad moved from Mecca to Yathrib(later Medina) to escape persecution by the Quraysh. This event established Islam as a religious and social order, which became the starting point of the Islamic calendar.
Encyclopedia Britannica Editors, 『The Britannica Guide to the Islamic World』, Agora, 2017, p43.

of wartime situations through migration, and even slavery and the kidnapping and violation of women. Therefore, until the Caliphate is restored, Islamic extremist fighters fearlessly justify and take for granted this struggle with the concept of holy jihad, in which Allah's will be fully accomplished.[37] In other words, it can be said that they are trying to transplant very dangerous values and systems to this land since they are justifying this with religious beliefs.

Accordingly, Abu Bakr al-Baghdadi[38], who presented the utopian goal for jihadists of establishing a caliphate, declared ISIS and reorganized the group to continue the fight against brutal terrorism in a more provocative and inflammatory manner. Then, many jihadists who were thirsty for real

---

[37] "These struggles are not temporary. Allah's authority must be established across the globe....."
Sayyid Qutb(2011), the book in front, p152.

[38] An Islamic cleric from Baghdad in Iraq, he formed an independent force with excellent organizational skills and tactics, established a Sunni caliphate in Iraq and Syria, and called himself the 'new caliph.'

struggle flocked to ISIS. They clearly showed their intention to transplant the country and system by carving out the Caliphate government system and issuing currency in units of the Caliphate era to build an economic system.[39] This has led to the admiration, support, and joining of many jihadists who are dreaming of restoring the caliphate state and transplanting the caliphate system to this land.[40] The 8,000-strong ISIS jihadists in the militia dare to declare that they will restore the Islamic Caliphate. At the base of their beliefs, it can be said that their seriousness lies in the fact that they contain a religious belief that they will risk even death and that they systemize this into a collective system.

---

39 "A large number of officials joined ISIS who had practically run the Iraqi government system for decades under the Saddam Hussein regime." , Nam Sik In, wisdom college, 2023.

40 While working in seclusion as an 'invisible leader,' he appeared as the 'new caliph Ibrahim' during Friday prayers at the Grand Mosque in Mosul and gathered followers.
Martin Chulov, The Guardian, 2014.07.06. "Abu Bakr al-Baghdadi emerges from shadows to rally Islamist followers"

3 Aliyah Movement, Jewish Zionism and Christianity, and the issue of establishing Jewish settlements in Palestine

One of the factors that contributed to this war was the establishment of illegal Jewish settlements in the Palestinian Region. The West Bank and Gaza-Israel borders were the minimum line to recognize each other's existence, which was made by agreement[41] between Israel, Palestine, and the International community. Jews are also people who have experienced the threat of ethnic cleansing in Europe and other places. But if they want to eliminate Palestinian Arabs while they return and establish their own country, this is an issue that Christians should think about carefully according to the Words of God, who wants to save all nations(Matthew

---

41 The current border was established after the 3rd Arab-Israeli war in 1967, and through the mediation of the U.S., Egypt and Israel signed the Camp David Agreement in 1978, and Israel and Palestine Liberation Organization(PLO) signed the Oslo Agreement in 1993.

24:14)**42** and the principles of the New Testament. As the Israeli government shifted to the right, they built illegal settlements in the Palestinian territories centered on Jewish converts from overseas, then attempted to protect themselves from friction with Palestine by sending security forces armed with guns. As the Hamas-Israel war progressed, an unstable situation continues in the West Bank. Jews who have settled in illegal settlements feel uneasy, shooting Palestinians, and protests by Palestinians in the West Bank against Israel continue.**43**

What is unusual is that many of Jews who have settled in

---

42 And this gospel of the kingdom will be preached in the whole world as a testimony to all nations, and then the end will come.

43 The international community's concerns are growing due to the expansion of illegal Jewish settlements and the influx of Jews based on Zionism. Israel has approved plans to build 5,700 new homes in the West Bank in the first half of 2023. About 13,000 houses have already been completed during the same period, which is three times the number of 2022. Accordingly, in June, four settlers were killed in a Palestinian attack, leading to continued violence against settlers. BBC NEWS, "Israel backs new Jewish settlement homes", 2013.08.11.
Yolande Knell, "West Bank: US 'troubled' by Israeli settlement expansion plans", BBC News, 2023.06.27.

illegal settlements are overseas immigrants who converted to Jews on the premise of observing the law and circumcision while abroad. This is deeply related to the Aliyah movement. For this purpose, local camps are opened in Nepal, China, Ukraine, Kazakhstan, and Sudan to convert even gentiles into Jews to make Gentile Jewish. And direct and indirect supporting movement is rising to return them to the land of Canaan in Israel. Inside Israel, the population density is already high, and those who have returned are encouraged to take root in illegal Jewish settlements in Palestinian territories.[44]

The Aliyah movement is an idea that was systemized in the situation of the Jews who were scattered during the Babylonian captivity in the Old Testament background because the Jews experienced the Babylonian captivity and thought that

---

[44] Among some Jews who participated in the Aliyah movement, there are cases where Protestants received support for immigrating to Israel. This appears to be a case of conversion to use Aliyah movement as a means of avoiding economic conditions in developing countries.
https://m.blog.naver.com/khchojh/222902469245

moving away from the temple was a curse and returning to their homeland near the temple and going up the Jerusalem temple was a blessing in the Old Testament. Meanwhile, there is a trend to support this movement in goodwill by Christians or churches who feel an affinity with the Old Testament background. But the idea of sanctifying the homeland of Israel and the tangible temple under the Aliyah movement is different from the Christian doctrine that, according to the New Testament, Jesus Christ became the temple in our hearts as believers, not in a tangible building or region. Additionally, Paul's view[45] in Romans that Jews will return to Jesus Christ after all the Gentiles have returned means that while the gospel is spreading among all nations, the plan of salvation remains for the Jewish people to accept as the Messiah. However, the Aliyah movement is a conversion movement that converts Gentiles into Jews by observing the law and circumcision; then

---

45 I do not want you to be ignorant of this mystery, brothers, so that you may not be conceited: Israel has experienced a hardening in part until the full number of the Gentiles has come in. And so all Israel will be saved. (Romans 11:25–26)

it is necessary to reflect on the Christian doctrine[46] that Paul warned against different gospel that said Gentiles must first become Jews by observing the law and circumcision before being saved during his mission to the Gentiles. Gentile ethnic peoples, such as those in Nepal, Sudan, etc., first become Jews through an initiation ceremony, observe the laws, and undergo circumcision to convert to Jews. Then, they accept Jewish religious doctrines. In addition, they can learn the anti-Christian religious beliefs that do not regard Jesus of Nazareth as their savior and wait for the Messiah based on Zionism who will bring national independence and political liberation to Israel. Of course, Jews can appreciate their goodwill and have friendly feelings toward Christians, as they helped in the movement to convert even Gentiles to Jews and return them to the Jewish homeland by providing enormous amounts of money and direct and indirect support. Nevertheless, it seems

---

[46] It is for freedom that Christ has set us free. Stand firm, then, and do not let yourselves be burdened again by a yoke of slavery. Mark my words! I, Paul, tell you that if you let yourselves be circumcised, Christ will be of no value to you at all. (Galatians 5:1–2)

there is a need for improvement in the massive amount of Christians' enthusiasm for investing in the Aliyah movement, which seeks to convert even Gentiles to Jews rather than Christians.

4 The possibility of refugee accommodation and refugee-oriented missions in countries adjacent to Israel and Palestine (Egypt, Jordan, and Lebanon) from a historical perspective.

1) Egypt

Egypt stands as the sole nation bordering the Palestine Gaza Strip while it is isolated on all sides due to the war, Israel's blockade of Gaza, Salami tactics[47] aimed at isolating Hamas, continuous airstrikes to destroy subterranean Hamas, and widespread devastation of the city. Furthermore, Egypt is also allowing border crossings for humanitarian aid activities and supplies from the international community. In such a case, will

---

[47] It is a negotiation tactic that subdivides a task into several stage and resolves them one by one, derived form the Italian sausage 'salami' which is eaten in thin slices.

Egypt, as a gesture of goodwill from a fellow Arab brotherhood country, or as the self-proclaimed head of the international Arab community, be willing to accommodate the over six million Palestinian refugees?[48] Unfortunately, the outlook is far from optimistic.

The current regime in Egypt led by Abdel Fattah Al Sisi is the group that ousted former President Mohamed Morsi from office through a military coup.[49] Morsi was known internationally as a president who came to power through popular vote during a period of political turmoil caused by significant civil unrest. However, behind the scenes, Morsi had his roots in the Muslim Brotherhood, of which he was

---

[48] Announcement of United Nations Relief and Works Agency for Palestine Refugees in the Near East(UNRWA), 2023

[49] Hyun Jung Ha, 「Egypt, A Return to the Old Issues of 'Bread, Freedom, Justice'」, 「The Arab Spring and Ten Years Thereafter」, sunpress, 2022 p.42-44.

the leader.[50] Hence, the incumbent president, stemming from a military background and responsible for the ousting of Morsi, along with his regime, is exhibiting apprehension or self-consciousness regarding the Muslim Brotherhood operating under Egypt's formidable influence to reclaim the regime through direct faction or personnel within their sphere of influence.

Since Hamas is the Palestinian branch of the Muslim Brotherhood and carries with it the ability to mobilize Arab-Islamic sentiments on issues such as Jerusalem and Israel, it is inevitable for the current regime to exercise greater vigilance than any past governments or regimes in monitoring the potential infiltration of Hamas operatives among the refugees permitted entry into Egypt. In other words, due to Hamas's adeptness at concealing and covering up its true nature within

---

[50] While a member of the Muslim Brotherhood, he was elected to the National Assembly as an independent party, but lost his seat due to repression by the Egyptian government in 2005, and was appointed as the leader of the Muslim Brotherhood.

the common Palestinian civil society, it is very improbable for Egypt to permit the entry of Palestinian refugees in hopes of preventing any possible influx of hidden Hamas leaders or operatives into its refugee community.[51] The assessment prevailing in the international community suggests that there have been significant concerns regarding the settlement of Palestinian refugees in Egypt, unrelated to the current Hamas conflict.[52] Therefore, the likelihood of the Egyptian government proactively accommodating refugees arising from the current crisis appears exceedingly low.

2) Jordan

---

[51] "Military-controlled countries in the Arab world, including Egypt, which receives economic support from the United States, are reluctant to join groups such as Hamas, believing that they will cause problems such as an Islamic revolution in their countries." Il Kwang Sung, 2023. https://youtu.be/syyO6bQNfF0?si=ArG0yqZSArZp7Jju

[52] Egypt has the authority to open the Rafah checkpoint, the only link between Gaza and the outside the world(excluding Israel). BBC News Korea. "What is the Rafah checkpoint on the Egyptian border, which has become the 'lifeline of Gaza Strip'?". 2023.11.02.

Jordan is a country that shares borders with the Palestinian West Bank, which has not yet been entirely swept by the war. Historically, just before the establishment of the Israeli government and the Palestinian Authority, there was a consciousness among the indigenous Palestinian Arab people that they belonged to the Transjordanian region.[53] Therefore, Jordan could be considered the top priority for refugee reception when Palestinian refugees occur. Nevertheless, Jordan has, historically, engaged in conflicts akin to civil war with the PLO (Palestine Liberation Organization)[54], which was

---

[53] Encyclopedia Britannica Editors, (2017), the book in front, p.198, 207.

[54] It is a secret resistance organization formed in 1964 with the goal of establishing an independent Palestine state. In Sep. 1993, it participated in the Oslo Accords on the autonomy of Israel, Gaza, and Jericho and is now transformed and legally existing as the Palestinian National Authority(PNA).

an antecedent stream to the Fatah Party[55] led by Yasser Arafat[56], who held authority over the West Bank region.[57] Though there were aspects of Arafat and the PLO transforming into a moderate faction as they entered into a peace agreement with Israel and turned away from the line of armed struggle during a period of lull, they originally pursued an armed struggle against Israel and relocated their operations to Jordan when they found themselves at a disadvantage.

However, the line of armed struggle between Arafat and the PLO against Israel ironically led to tensions and antagonism with the Jordanian government, which had initially provided

---

[55] An important political party of the PLO, organized under the leadership of Yasser Arafat on Jan. 1st, 1957.

[56] He was the first head of the PLO and chairman of the PNA and led the Palestinian independence struggle for over 40 years. A symbol of resistance against Israel and a national hero of Palestine, he received conflicting evaluations during his lifetime as both a freedom fighter and a terrorist. In 1994, he won the Nobel Peace Prize along with Israel's Yitzhak Rabin and Shimon Peres.

[57] During a period known as Black September, Arafat ordered the overthrow of the "fascist government" of Jordan's King Hussein. BBC News, "1970: Civil war breaks out in Jordan"

them refuge and a base for their operations. This situation eventually escalated into conflicts between the Arab brother nations – Jordan and the PLO, where they found themselves at gunpoint. Consequently, Jordan expelled Arafat and the PLO from its territory.[58]

Given such historical experiences, the Jordanian government, while referring to Palestinians as brethren, finds itself compelled to exercise extreme caution regarding the potential influx of Hamas intertwined with Palestinian refugees. This caution stems from Hamas still maintaining an armed struggle stance as they settle in Jordan as exiles or refugees after losing ground in Palestine. Hence, the possibility of Jordan proactively accommodating refugees from the Gaza Strip is likewise extremely slim.

---

[58] In early 1971, Arafat and the PLO were expelled from Jordan. Pierre Tristam, "Black September: The Jordanian-PLO Civil War of 1970", ThoughtCo., 2019.07.03.

3) Lebanon

Lebanon, compared to Jordan, as previously mentioned, suffered more severely from the historical wound of being engulfed in civil war while allowing Arafat, who was expelled from Jordan, to use southern Lebanon as the major base for armed struggles against Israel.[59] Lebanon, uniquely, has a republican form of government but with a peculiar national structure where power is decentralized among religious sects, such as the Maronite Christians, Sunni Muslims, and Shia Muslims, based on their respective proportions within the population. Within this framework of sectarian power-sharing in the Lebanese government, Arafat's establishment of a stronghold in southern Lebanon not only provoked friction

---

[59] Clashes between the Lebanese Christian faction and PLO guerrillas(who came to Lebanon in the 1970s) with Palestinian militias, led to a civil war that lasted for 15 years from 1975. This civil war resulted in more than 100,000 deaths.
Kyung Soo Lee, 「Lebanon, A People's Cry for a Mosaic Society and Unity」, 『The Arab Spring and Ten Years Thereafter』, sunpress, 2022 p.156.

and clashes against Israel but also within Lebanon, leading to the emergence of factional armed militias along sectarian lines, consequently triggering a prolonged civil war.[60]

In the impoverished southern region of Lebanon, which Arafat utilized as a refuge and a base for the struggle against Israel, the Shia community, relatively marginalized from government power-sharing arrangements, constituted the majority. Seizing upon this state of neglect and turmoil, Hezbollah[61] emerged as a vigorous armed force supported by external patrons, primarily led by the Shia community. After establishing an Islamic Shia

---

60 "Lebanese society, based on sectarianism, gave birth to clientelism. This type of clientelism makes citizens swear allegiance to sect leaders rather than the state, making easy for each sect leader to incite the people to blindly follow them."
Kyung Soo Lee, the book in front, p157–160.

61 It is a Lebanese Islamic Shia armed force and political party founded in 1983. Following the Iranian Shia Revolution in 1979 and the Israeli invasion in 1982, a group of Lebanese Shia clerics formed Hezbollah with the goal of expelling Israel from Lebanon and establishing an Islamic state there.
Encyclopedia Britannica Editors, (2017), the book in front, p245.

theocratic fundamentalism regime in Iran in 1979[62], Ayatollah Khomeini supported the Shia community within Lebanon in 1982, instigating the establishment of Hezbollah, which aimed to expel Israel from Lebanon under the mandate of jihad, bestowing upon it the name Hezbollah, meaning 'Party of God, Islamic Jihad.'[63] This is essentially the trend of Islamic extremism, and the system emphasized in this text, which is also similar to the form of coordination between discrete organizations.

The expansion of the northern front of Israel due to Hezbollah has become a matter of great concern in the international community. Hezbollah, having engaged in prolonged conflicts supporting fraternal Shia armed groups in the form of discrete organizations within the Syrian civil

---

[62] "In a tenured position, the highest religious leader intervenes in the President, Cabinet, and National Assembly through the Constitution Guard Committee under Islamic law.", Nam Sik In, 2022, https://youtu.be/0dv_vZR1oL_Q?si=m4fIMeZUZfWhdmiz

[63] "Iran also tried to spread its type of movement, the Islamic Revival Movement, to neighboring Islamic countries." , Encyclopedia Britannica Editors, (2017), the book in front, p233.

war for over a decade,[64] appears unlikely to initiate a full-scale confrontation with Israel first. On the other hand, amid the ongoing sporadic missile skirmishes between Israel and Hezbollah, if Israel asserts its dominance against Hamas, it cannot entirely exclude the possibility of engaging in a full-scale confrontation with Lebanon and Hezbollah.[65]

In this way, the unsettled sporadic frontlines cast a shadow over Lebanon's capacity to accommodate refugees. Furthermore, considering the historical scars of turmoil and civil war that were caused by past instances when Arafat and

---

[64] Hezbollah is a staunch ally of Syria President Bashar al-Assad, who sent thousands of armed fighters for President Assad when the Syrian civil war intensified in 2011.
BBC News Korea, "Who is the Lebanese armed group Hezbollah?", 2023.10.18.,

[65] On Jan. 2nd and 8th, Israel killed senior Hezbollah official Saleh al-Arouri and commander Wissam al-Towil in airstrikes. Additionally, during a recent interview with Yoav Gallant(retired Israeli military general), he emphasized that "what is happening in Gaza could be 'copy-pasted' to Beirut."
Dario Sabaghi, "Are Hezbollah and Israel edging closer to war?", THE NEW ARAB, 2024.01.15
Laila Bassam and Maya Gebeily, "Israeli strike kills a Hezbollah commander in Lebanon", REUTERS, 2024.01.09.

the PLO used Lebanon as a base for armed resistance against Israel before opting for a moderate approach, it is unlikely that Lebanon will be inclined to accommodate Palestinian refugees indiscriminately along with Hamas.

5 Conclusion & Forecast

Hamas started as a branch of the Palestinian Muslim Brotherhood. It was implanted with the undertone of the system transplantation, which is aimed at establishing the caliphate system of the Egyptian Muslim Brotherhood's Hassan al-Banna. Therefore, Hamas has the form of a political party and transplantation of the government system. At the same time, it also resembles the network of movements that Hassan al-Banna used to operate over 500 branches of discrete organizations across the country and throughout the Muslim world. Hamas not only exists in Palestine but also has branches and discrete organizations in Qatar, Turkey, etc. Like many modern Islamic extremism movement organizations (influenced by Qutb, the second leader of the Muslim Brotherhood), Hamas promotes terrorism as an armed strike line and asymmetric warfare across civil society and front lines and, thus, is trying to confront the powerful nation of Israel. However, it is difficult to say that Hamas has a wide range of networks around the world, like Osama Bin Laden's Al Qaeda. Additionally, Hamas shows aspects of system transplantation as ISIS. However, ISIS disillusioned the world with Islamic extremism by attempting to implant a malignant system of Muhammad's early caliphate history with the prototype form, including terrorism, kidnapping, and public executions. Also, ISIS had tied up about 8,000 jihadists in one area. Rather than a form of an asymmetrical conflict between a powerful country and a borderless frontline of discrete organization, the confrontation between system and system led to chaos as a result. But Hamas is subtly different from them.

Hamas is an implantation of the political party regime. However, (despite its own corruption) it is an election-based regime that had to gain support based on public opinion by taking on the role of a delivery channel of international relief goods, etc. Although Hamas has the motive of implanting the system of ISIS, it also has the aspect of sympathizing, building on, and appealing to the opinion of certain people in the Arabic region. Hezbollah's armed political party, also has the aspect of appealing to, soliciting, and sympathizing with local public sentiment to the extent of producing members of Congress.[66] In this sense, it is highly likely that Hamas' self-reliance as a system will last longer than the volatile collapse of a malicious system such as ISIS.

Extremism movements and discrete organization-type principles linked to systems such as the Houthi rebels, Hezbollah, and Hamas are growing their own on several continents with

---

[66] After producing eight members of the National Assembly in 1992, it has participated in the cabinet as a major political party since 2005. In the 2022 general election, 13 seats were maintained.
Kali Robinson, Council on Foreign Relations, "What is Hezbollah? What to know about its origins, structure and history", PBS NEWS HOUR, 2023.10.16.

getting some public will by appealing to local communities.[67] Among them, if it has discrete organization network mobility and direct or indirect linkage with the Arab world in Islamic extremism systems and networks, it will have strengths and weaknesses in the mixed aspects of Islamic fundamentalism and extremist organizations that were highlighted in the past, such as Al-Qaeda and ISIS. Then, there is a possibility of creating an era of waves with new trends in extremism. If these mixed Islamic political factions and extremist organizations have been established longer than ISIS and created systems where each operates locally based on discrete organizations(although they do not reach the discrete organization mobility of Al-Qaeda), and there is loose solidarity with each other over a common issue that hostile to Israel like Hamas, Hezbollah, and Houthi rebels, it could cause significant repercussions, confusion, and conflict in the Middle East world. In other words, unlike

---

[67] Houthi rebel leaders are well-versed in the tribal system of Yemen and have secured many tribal allies by utilizing the network of former President Saleh.
ACLED, "Increasing tribal resistance to Houthi rule", reliefweb, 2019.03.07.

the precedent[68] of implanting ISIS's malicious system that is volatilized and devastated the surrounding area like cancer cells, it appears that they can continue to establish themselves that are unlikely to collapse in a short period of time.

Unfortunately, the prospects for approaching ministry to Palestinian refugees are not bright, as mentioned above in the article. Nevertheless, when predicting an increase in the liquidity of the Middle East conflict in the future, it is necessary to approach the ministry sufficiently until the point when the road is open for refugee ministry in places such as Jordan, including existing Syrian refugees. It is difficult to predict when and in which region instability will increase in the Middle East due to this mixed pattern of extremism. Refugees are people who have left their homeland due to instability, and they are

---

68 Action is urgently needed for the civilians detained under ISIS—occupied territory and the more than 8,000 missing people. And if ISIS fighters remain uncontrolled, they may cause chaos in Syria and pose a serious threat to Iraq.
Simon Tisdall, "The collapse of Isis will inflame the regional power struggle", The Guardian, 2019.02.17.

people who have broken away from an Islamic totalitarian society and can move to a place where they can make their own choices. So, the current refugee ministry in the Middle East must focus more on open areas. Instability within the Arab world is increasing due to the mixing of Islamic extreme political factions and discrete organizations, and unpredictable conflicts in the Middle East may emerge in unexpected way in each regions. Therefore, the best Christian capabilities should be invested where the ministry is open with the attitude that opportunities and periods for refugee ministry may be limited.

The flow of **extremism in the Middle East** seen through **the Israel-Hamas war**

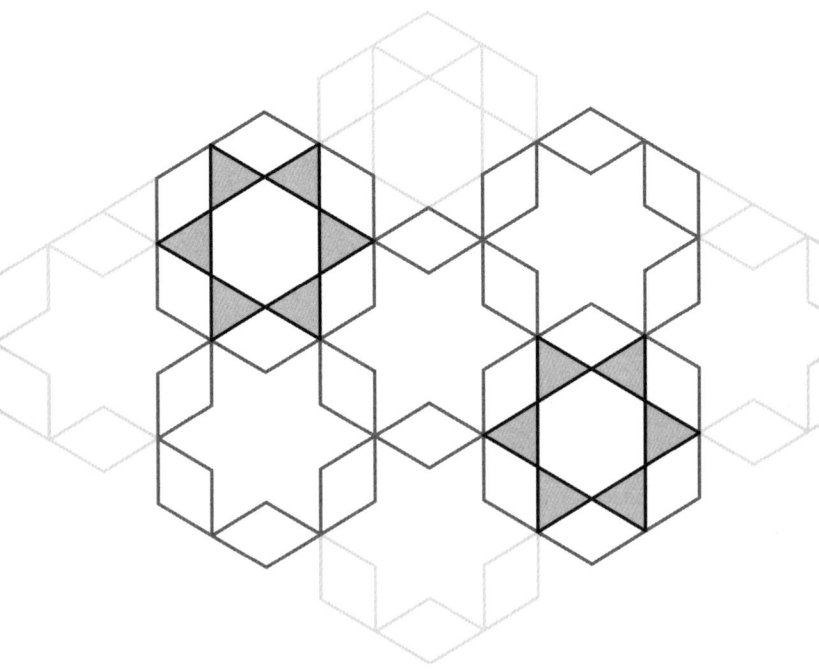

2

The origins and research tasks of the Arab - the remaining nation, Timely situational analysis

- Focusing on Arab tribalism

1 Raising Questions about the Origins of Arabs
- Pondering the roots of Arab tribalism

The Origins of Arabs are often strangely overlooked, or their pre-7th century history is treated inadequately in Middle Eastern Studies, Islamic Studies, and Arabic Studies. Despite the immense influence of Arabs, who spread Islam to the Middle East, North Africa, Central Asia, and Southeast Asia, their origins and roots are often curiously disregarded by historians both within and outside the Arab world. In most historical presentations of Arabs, their historiography began in earnest from the 7th century onwards, following the systematization of the Islamic religion. The Arab people have existed since before the 7th century. So why is there a strong tendency to overlook the origins of the Arab people in the history of Islamic and Middle Eastern studies, which originated in Arabia?

From the perspective of Arabic studies, there are authoritative figures who have had a profound impact on Arab history or established historical perspectives, such as Muhammad and Ibn Khaldun,[1] who were insiders in the Arab world. From the perspective of Arabic studies, authoritative figures who have had a profound impact on Arab history or established historical perspectives, such as Muhammad and Ibn Khaldun, were insiders in the Arab world. It acknowledged widely that Muhammad, the founder of Islam, exerted a profound influence on Arab history. However, he also disparaged the pre-Islamic Arab era as a period of ignorance and

---

[1] A 14th-century Tunisian Islamic historian, thinker, and statesman, he systematized the first sociological insights into the turbulent politics and society of North Africa at the time. Through his objective and critical analysis, which differed from the traditional Islamic historiography of the time, he attempted to shed light on the nature of history, the process of historical change, and the general laws of the flow of human history. His major works include the Muqaddimah(An Introduction to History, History of Islamic Thought, 1377).
Song Kyung-Keun, 「A Study on the Asabiyah of Ibn Khaldun」, 『Collection of writings of Korean Association Of The Middle East Studies』 Book No.36, Ch.3, p.69-92, 2016.

barbarity known as the Jahiliyha,[2] thereby overshadowing the rich history of Arabia before the advent of Islam. This perspective impacted significantly subsequent historians, including Ibn Khaldun, who approached Arab history from an internal Islamic and Middle Eastern perspective. As a result, the narrative of Arab history has largely absorbed into post-7th century Islamic historiography, with the pre-Islamic period often relegated to a cursory introduction.[3]

In addition, there are significant limitations in the perspectives of Western academic authorities on Arab Islamic history, such as Bernard Lewis and Hans Kung, who overlook aspects of pre-7th century Arabia. It is because the West, represented by the Byzantine Empire founded by the Hellas after the Romans,

---

2 Derived from the Arabic word for 'ignorance.' A state of affairs that existed before the emergence of Islam.

3 "There must be a clear distinction between life in the pre-Islamic era of Jahiliyyah and life as a Muslim. Only when one has completely severed ties with Jahiliyyah can one truly embrace Islam.", Sayyid Qutb, Translated by Jung Min Seo, 『Milestones』, Pyung Sa Li, 2011, p.73

primarily encountered Arabs after the 7th century, when it had transformed into Islamic systematization.[4]

2 Beyond Research Constraints
- The absence of records of Arab nomadic culture and the Utilization of Islamic Intellectual Archives Injected with Hellenic Intellect

As such, there are significant aspects of Arab origins overlooked from the perspectives of these authorities who have shaped the paradigm of Arab history, regardless of whether they are from the West or the Middle East. Additionally, Arabs had a nomadic lifestyle before the Islamization of the religion, resulting in a weak[5] culture of recording sedentary life.

---

4 Jeon Wan Gyung, 「Arab Cultural History」, Korean Studies Information, 2013, p.42

5 Jeon Wan Gyung, the Book in front, p.18~20
Hans Kung, 「Hans Kung Islam」, Siwajinsil, 2012, p.80-84

Consequently, the lack of records of pre-Islamic Arabia makes it challenging to study the origins of Arabs and their pre-Islamic history. However, Islam borrowed heavily from the narratives of the Old and New Testaments, resulting in significant internal contradictions within the Quran that cannot be compared to the internal coherence and unity of the Bible. In this sense, there was an aspect of Islam attempting to fill the contradictions of its scriptures with the apologetics of Hellenic thought. Ironically, this opened the door for the infusion of Hellenic thought into Islamic society, leading to the accumulation of intellectual knowledge through the establishment of various libraries and academies throughout the Arab Mediterranean region.[6] Therefore, it would be beneficial if someone who is a field researcher, theorist, and missionary and could open a new academic paradigm take on the challenge of academic systemization of the origin and introduction of Arabia, as well as its pre-Islamic history by utilizing the relatively accurate

---

6 Encyclopedia Britannica Editors, 『The Britannica Guide to the Islamic World』, Agora, 2017, p.74~85

oral tradition of Arab, and the intellectual archives that systematically preserved in Arab society through the encounter with Hellenism after Islam. The study of the origins of Arabia and its pre-Islamic history is a crucial and potentially transformative field for understanding the true nature of the Middle East. However, due to the reasons mentioned above, it remains largely unexplored academically, akin to uncharted territory. While extensive scholarly research has been conducted on Middle Eastern Arabia from antiquity to the present day, this area remains a frontier for exploration, with the potential to revolutionize academic paradigms and open up new avenues of inquiry if its research findings are validated.

3 The Origins of Arabs in the Bible
- The Arab lineage traces back to Ishmael and Muhammad

Surprisingly, Arabs refer to the Southern Arabs

centered in Saudi Arabia as 'Qahtan' but do not consider them as the bloodline and spiritual lineage of Ishmael and Muhammad. Instead, they refer to the Northern Arabs as 'Adnan' and consider them as the bloodline and spiritual lineage of Ishmael and Muhammad.[7] It is clear from the Old Testament that Ishmael was banished from Abraham's lineage and that Hagar, an Egyptian, was lost in the desert near the Egyptian border and headed south to Arabia.[8] Then why do Arabs themselves consider the northern Arabs to be their bloodline descendants of Ishmael Muhammad? Generally, Arabs have a clear lineage that is passed down through their family line to the point where their names are identified by their family and who their father is. Ultimately, the roots of this lineage can be traced back to the Bible and the marriage of Ishmael, the ancestor of the Arabs, to a daughter of Esau. The Bible reveals the identity and origin of the northern Arabs, recording the marriage of

---

7 Jeon Wan Gyung, the Book in front, p.22~25

8 While he was living in the Desert of Paran, his mother got a wife for him from Egypt.(Genesis 21:21)

Ishmael's daughter to Esau (Genesis 25:13, 28:9).[9] Additionally, the descendants of Ishmael's second son, Kedar, and other branches flourished in the north and are mentioned alongside Arabia (Isaiah 60:6-7, Ezekiel 27:20-22).[10]

Thus, the northern Arabs formed from this lineage, and they can be found today in Jordan, Lebanon, Syria, Palestine, and other places. Among these northern Arabs, Muhammad,

---

9 These are the names of the sons of Ishmael, listed in the order of their birth: Nebaioth the firstborn of Ishmael, Kedar, Adbeel, Mibsam,(Genesis 25:13)
so he went to Ishmael and married Mahalath, the sister of Nebaioth and daughter of Ishmael son of Abraham, in addition to the wives he already had.(Genesis 28:9)

10 Herds of camels will cover your land, young camels of Midian and Ephah. And all from Sheba will come, bearing gold and incense and proclaiming the praise of the LORD. All Kedar's flocks will be gathered to you, the rams of Nebaioth will serve you; they will be accepted as offerings on my altar, and I will adorn my glorious temple.(Isaiah 60:6–7)
Dedan traded in saddle blankets with you. Arabia and all the princes of Kedar were your customers; they did business with you in lambs, rams and goats. The merchants of Sheba and Raamah traded with you; for your merchandise they exchanged the finest of all kinds of spices and precious stones, and gold.(Ezekiel 27:20–22)

the founder of Islam, was born. Therefore, even Arab society today recognizes that the bloodline of Ishmael-Muhammad is not based on the southern Arabs of Saudi Arabia but on the northern Arabs.

4 Research on Arab origins and redefinition of research categories for introductory Arabic studies, Middle Eastern studies, and Islamic studies
- Including the North Africa region, Central Asia region, and Southeast Asia region

According to the Bible, the origins of Arabs can be traced back to the marriage between Ishmael's daughter and Esau and the lineage of Ishmael's other sons, including the lineage of Kedar. It led to the development of the broader group of

Northern Arabs, culminating in the lineage of Muhammad, the founder of Islam. Thus, the genealogical roots of Arabs and the lineage of the founder of Islam can be found in this biblical narrative. Distinguishing systematic Arabic that leads up to the Arab origin and the emergence of Islam leads one to consider the need to recategorize the introductory category of academic studies of many regions that have been influenced by Arab-Islam. Of course, those regions greatly influenced by Arab Islam include the Middle East, North Africa, Central Asia, and Southeast Asia. Even so, the scope of the study and the criteria for dividing them were unclear whether they were based on Arab ancestry, linguistic compatibility, Islamic religious spirituality, or geopolitical location.

The concept of the Middle East emerged in response to the Western-centric geopolitical concept of the Near East. Therefore, the terms "Middle East studies" and "Middle East region" are vague geopolitical concepts that fail to capture the unique characteristics of Arab-Islam despite being the core region where Arab and Islamic civilizations originated.[11]

As previously mentioned, Arabs can be divided into two main groups based on their lineage and ethnicity: Northern Arabs and Southern Arabs, both tracing their ancestry back to Ishmael and Muhammad. However, while Northern Arabs hold the bloodline, Southern Arabia has played a central role in shaping the Arab identity since the 7th century. It is because Islam originated in Southern Arabia, centered around Mecca and Medina, and continues to exert its strong religious influence from Saudi Arabia.[12]

If so, on what basis is the scope of study of North African Arabs, Central Asia, and Southeast Asian Islam divided? Is it divided by a geopolitical concept like the Middle East? Is it divided by the concept of Arabs as a bloodline-based ethnic unit?

---

[11] Nam Sik In(Professor in Korea National Diplomatic Academy), 2022. https://www.youtube.com/watch?v=FHcm7B_VjVE

[12] Jeon Wan Gyung, the Book in front, p.33-34

Or is it divided based on the religious spirituality of Islam? The criteria are vague. North Africa is often vaguely conceptualized as "Arab North Africa" due to its Islamic influence. But Central Asia, despite also being an Islamically influenced region, is not conceptualized or studied under the same umbrella term of "Arab Central Asia" in academic discourse. If so, does it mean the North African region is Arab in terms of bloodline and ethnicity just because it was influenced by Islam? Why is the term 'Arab' used for North Africa when there is almost no bloodline connection to North African people, as there is for Southern and Northern Arabs? It seems that 'Arab' in North Africa is a concept distinguished by linguistic commonality. In contrast to Central Asia, which was also Islamized, the current North African region continues to use and employ Modern Standard Arabic as its public language.[13] Therefore, the term "Arab" in the context of the "Arab" world of North Africa is not a distinction based on bloodline, tribe, ethnicity, or religious

---

13 A Moroccan professor argues that "Arabism is essentially language and culture.", Jeon Wan Gyung, the Book in front, p.36

identity but rather a distinction based on the shared language of Modern Standard Arabic.

Meanwhile, Central Asia and Southeast Asia came under the influence of Islam, and the Quran spread in Arabic, bringing them under the sphere of influence of Arabic script. However, they did not adopt Arabic as their common language, as did North Africa. Therefore, the concepts of 'Central Asian Arab' and 'Southeast Asian Arab' are not as common as 'North African Arab.'

In conclusion, a more precise and consistent framework for the scope of academic research and categorization criteria is required for Middle Eastern, Arab, Islamic, North African Arab, Central Asian, and Southeast Asian Islamic studies. It is rare for a field of study to have such a mixed scope of academic research, combining geopolitical, linguistic, genealogical/ethnic, and religious concepts without established criteria for academic consensus. The research on the Arabic origins stemming from the Bible seems to have been overlooked or left incomplete, only described in terms of the Islamic expansion after the 7th century and its geopolitical impact on encounters with the West. It gives the impression that the first paragraph is vaguely inserted.

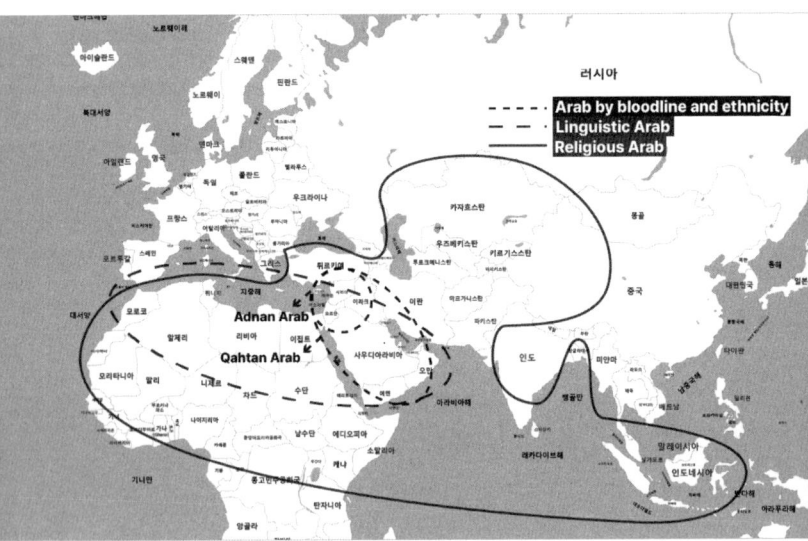

5 Arab Root Tribalism, Muhammad, and Israel Hamas War and Peace Solutions

In light of the recent Israel-Hamas conflict, particularly in the West, there has been a renewed interest in federalism as a solution. Previously, the two-state solution[14] (Israel and Palestine coexisting as separate states) and the one-state solution[15] (a single state with Israel at its core) were proposed as solutions by the international community. However, neither of these solutions has been feasible in practice. Federalism, as proposed here, suggests an alternative approach: a loose confederation of Israel and Palestine, recognizing the self-determination of both parties, similar to the United States. The view that a one-state solution is like a whole marriage, a two-

---

14 Two-state solution, The establishment of a Jewish state of Israel and a Palestinian state for the Palestinian people as a solution to the Israeli-Palestinian conflict was part of the Oslo Accords of 1993. Britannica, https://www.britannica.com/topic/two-state-solution

15 One state solution, Yousef Munayyer (Secretary-General of the Jerusalem Fund for Palestinian Center) argued for 'the establishment of a constitution that guarantees equal rights for Palestinians, overcoming the past through truth-seeking and reparations, and establishing a single state.', Foreign Affairs, 2019.

state solution is like a divorce, and a federal-state solution[16] is like a consensual cohabitation has been advocated in the international community. However, this view is simply borrowing the motifs of the Western system and is an attempt to resolve this extreme conflict in a self-serving manner without fully understanding the roots and characteristics of the Middle East and Arab society.

The ancient conflict[17] between Ishmael and Isaac, which forms the basis of the modern Arab-Israeli conflict in the Middle East, is actually rooted in the ancient Middle Eastern law and its heritage of "an eye for an eye, a tooth for a tooth" and the blood feuds and tribal resentments that persisted in the region for generations. It is a legacy rooted in the pre-Islamic

---

16 Dr. Mordechai Kedar's plan (Palestinian Emirates Plan, Eight-state solution) proposes a UAE-style federation of seven major tribes in the West Bank, with international support for its establishment, Nam Sik In, 2018.

17 But Sarah saw that the son whom Hagar the Egyptian had borne to Abraham was mocking, and she said to Abraham, "Get rid of that slave woman and her son, for that slave woman's son will never share in the inheritance with my son Isaac. (Genesis 21:9–10)

Arab world, long before Islam was systematized. However, even Muhammad was unable to overcome this prototype of Arab tribalism. Muhammad united the tribes under the concept of monotheism, calling the pre-Islamic society characterized by tribal conflicts and social division "Jahiliyyah." However, even Muhammad could not escape the web of grudges and feuds inherent in Arabian tribalism. After migrating from Mecca to Medina, he took revenge on the Arab Jews who had disregarded his claim to prophethood, massacring them mercilessly and enslaving their women and children. This act of vengeance fueled their resentment, leading to his eventual assassination by poisoning, marking the end of Muhammad's life.

Therefore, the Middle Eastern Arab legal inheritance tradition of "an eye for an eye, a tooth for a tooth" serves as the foundation for interpreting Arab society today. To naively interpret the extreme confrontation between Israel, Hamas, Palestine, and Arab Islamic society during the Israel-Hamas War through a simple Western lens and attribute it to structural factors is to overlook the roots of Arab society. The blood feud relationships of Arab tribalism are more fundamental and take precedence over systems, governments, and religion. Therefore, the war between Israel and Hamas will only deepen the tribal grudge, and it cannot be resolved through the system, governance structure, containment and proposals of international organizations. Only by overcoming the demands of the law and the complete gospel of forgiveness and the message of reconciliation can peace be possible.

6 Examining the Arab Spring through the Lens of Arab Islamic Tribalism[18]

1) Cause of the Libyan Civil War - Islamic Tribalism

The end of Muammar Gaddafi,[19] the former dictator of Libya, was gruesome. Gaddafi enjoyed using the title "King of Kings," which was an expression commonly self-proclaimed

---

18 This article was written shortly after the Middle East uprisings in 2011.

19 The head of state in Libya, the dictator who ruled Libya for 42 years, the longest in the world as of 2011. The Libyan Revolution, which began on February 15, 2011, with anti-government democracy protests in Benghazi, the second largest city in Libya, escalated into tribal conflict and resulted in numerous casualties, ending with Gaddafi's death on October 20.

by kings when they ended chaos during the archaic tribal era.[20] Gaddafi, who reveled in the somewhat anachronistic title of "King," ruled with absolute power but ultimately fell victim to the grudges between tribes. In defining Middle Eastern uprisings as democratization, the West is committing a self-contradictory and circular error. Accepting the Western model of democratization as the cause and effect of large-scale social unrest in the Middle East and, therefore, intervening with force and hegemony is self-contradictory. Moreover, the West's understanding and schematization of the Middle East are also highly egocentric and simplistic. These behaviors have become the seed of the tragic conflicts between the Middle East and the West for many years.[21]

---

[20] During his speech at the 2009 UN General Assembly, Gaddafi referred to himself as the 'King of Kings of Africa'.
Africanews with United Nations, "Muammar Gaddafi at the 64th UN General Assembly in 2009", Africanews, 2019.09.12., https://www.africanews.com/2017/09/19/speech-muammar-gaddafi-at-the-64th-un-general-assembly-in-2009/

[21] Nam Sik In, 「The Arab Spring that thwarted the ideals of international politics」, 「The Arab Spring and Ten Years Thereafter」, snupress, 2022, p.247-250.

Can the contrasting behaviors of Libyans following the overthrow of dictator Gaddafi be simply explained by a desire for Western-style democracy? On one hand, some Libyans remained loyal to Gaddafi even to the bitter end, blinded by misguided devotion. On the other hand, there were those who, despite being bribed by Gaddafi's immense hidden wealth, relentlessly pursued and brutally killed the ousted leader. Can this extreme difference in madness be attributed solely to a yearning for Western-style democracy?[22] Can the civil war between Libyans, divided between those who supported and those who sought to overthrow Gaddafi, be simply categorized as a conflict of systems stemming from religion, politics, or ethnic ideology? Before the deliberate imposition of systems, there existed naturally occurring tribes. The concept of tribes predates the emergence of Western hegemony as a single system encompassing religion, politics, and economy.

---

[22] Human Rights Watch(International non-governmental organization) https://www.hrw.org/report/2012/10/16/death-dictator/bloody-vengeance-sirte

Therefore, it is more accurate to view tribal fragmentation as a code of the ancient world rather than a phenomenon unfolding in modern times. This is because the victory of a centralized system, which can effectively concentrate and deploy power, over a decentralized, fragmented tribal system is a distinctly Western and modern phenomenon.[23]

Arab Islam is historically a product of the intersection between the tribal and religious systems. Before the 7th century AD, during the lifetime of Muhammad,[24] the Arabian Peninsula was nothing more than a periphery on the margins of Middle Eastern hegemony. At that time, the state of the Middle East was like an empty vessel that had fed on the nourishment of Christianity. There was a wiggling desire to revive the heyday of the Eastern Roman Empire and the old

---

[23] Amy Chua, Translated by Seung Jin Kim, 『Political Tribes: Group Instinct and the Fate of Nation』, Bookie, 2020, p.79-81.

[24] Muslims usually call him al-Rasul(the Messenger) and Rasul Allah(the Messenger of Allah). He is the founder of Islam.

empire, which was already decrepit as the age of civilization, but the constant conflict with the Persian Empire was continuing tediously, which lacked deep religious nourishment such as the spirituality of Christianity[25]. This destructive energy did not provide new dynamism to the human community but became a confrontation between imperial systems that aligned their forces according to the laws of hegemony. And at that time, there seemed to be no power or civilizational alternative to oppose them.

Muhammad, determined to reshape the Arabian Peninsula, emerged with his monotheistic ideology and a social order centered on the Arabs amid this tumultuous clash of civilizations in the Middle East. While the surrounding regions of the Middle East were embroiled in conflicts between aging civilizations, the interior of the primitive Arabian Peninsula was plagued by constant strife and discord among its tribal societies. The tribal worldview of the Arabian Peninsula was

---

[25] Encyclopedia Britannica Editors, 『The Britannica Guide to the Islamic World』, Agora, 2017, p.107–111.

highly insular and cohesive within groups based on kinship or tribal affinity, but once conflict and hostility arose with another group, it would lead to generations of enmity between them.[26]

Muhammad, as a merchant, traveled long distances for his trades. During his trips, he encountered the concept of monotheism and was captivated by the biblical narrative[27] of the Old Testament introduced by non-mainstream Christians and diaspora[28] Jews he interacted with. Muhammad saw the constant chaos and hostility within Arabian tribal society as a direct consequence of their religious impiety. He fervently called for the rejection of the various idols worshipped by the different tribes. Muhammad attributed the incessant conflicts,

---

26 Encyclopedia Britannica Editors(2017), the book in front, p.34-42.

27 It is a word derived from the Latin verb 'narrare,' meaning 'to speak,' and has a similar meaning to storytelling. It is used as a concept that encompasses not only the depiction of true or fictional events but also various strategies and forms used to organize and develop the story.

28 Initially, it was a term referring to the ethnic separation of Jews, but in modern times, it has been expanded and used as a general term for refugees, people, and their descendants who were forced to leave their homeland due to war and colonization.

chaos, and hostility among the tribes in Arabia to the divisions and curses brought about by polytheism. He sought to break down tribal boundaries and establish unity in the Arabian Peninsula through the propagation of monotheism.

But Muhammad could only incorporate inaccurate biblical information and monotheistic concepts from Christianity and Judaism, still bound by tribal values and their influence. Even he felt the contempt expressed by the Arabian diaspora Jewish tribes who considered him a heretical self-proclaimed prophet and mercilessly massacred and exterminated them after they surrendered during the war. On one occasion, a Jewish woman, whose tribe had been decimated by Muhammad, attempted to assassinate him by serving him poisoned lamb, disguised as a gesture of hospitality. Muhammad unknowingly took a bite and, sensing something foul, quickly spat out the food, narrowly escaping death. From that point on, whenever he fell ill throughout his life, even on his deathbed, he attributed his declining health to the poisoning attempt. He lived the rest of his life consumed by resentment over the assassination attempt.

In reality, he embraced and tolerated most of the tribal customs and practices as long as they did not oppose the monotheism of Allah.[29]

As Muhammad conquered the Middle East by force under the banner of Islam and tribal unification, Islam was established as a religious system on a foundation that directly reflected his tribal customs and remained firmly entrenched in the Middle East to this day. Like layers of moss that have accumulated over time, Islam possessed strong centripetal force and came to have distinct differences from other religious, political, and economic systems that have reorganized their members according to their shared values and uniform lifestyles. While Islam established a single religious system throughout the Middle East, it also allowed and encouraged divisive and exclusive tribalism. Other

---

29 Encyclopedia Britannica Editors(2017), the book in front, p.45-50.

systems, unlike Islam, are mostly hostile toward tribalism[30] and prefer to dismantle it, either radically or gradually, rather than coexist with it.

As an example, it is obvious that a king who establishes a centralized political system is uncomfortable with tribal divisions. The Pope, who upheld a single faith and the Catholic tradition, naturally did not delight in the closed nature of tribal blood ties. Those who believed in an efficient economic system and the economic theorists who supported it wanted to create a general and economic centripetal force for production and distribution through predictable and schematizable economic phenomena. They were less interested in the various forms of self-sufficiency within each tribe. Also, the intersection of tribalism and the system in Middle Eastern Islam is distinct

---

[30] Generally, it is an ideology that pursues a group of people with homogeneous traditions, ancestors, language, culture, religion, etc. The ideal is a state that is small, relatively isolated and has a low degree of political integration. In most cases, the goal is a tribal system in which there is no centralized political power.

from both the ancient tribal societies in Africa and the rational systems in the West. Therefore, understanding the Libyan civil war must begin with an understanding of the internal dynamics of Arab Islam. In fact, it was the resistance of the hostile tribes against Gaddafi, who ruled like a monarch, that served as the driving force behind the popular overthrow of the Libyan dictatorship. This is because, for Arabs who prioritize tribal lineage and honor over state law, even someone with absolute power like Gaddafi would uncompromisingly become an irreconcilable enemy if they belonged to a hostile tribe. While the primary cause of Gaddafi's brutal killing must be attributed to his tyranny, it is impossible to arrive at a complete diagnosis without understanding the Libyan situation in light of the tribal conflict patterns.[31]

Libya currently faces a perilous challenge. While Gaddafi was undoubtedly a dangerous figure, the tribes were armed and empowered in the absence of a suitable central authority

---

[31] Encyclopedia Britannica Editors(2017), the book in front, p.434-438.

or power to replace his regime. This would likely lead to tribes acting based on ancient codes of clan-based patronage relationships. They may also recognize any emerging regime only insofar as it strengthens their tribal positions. However, Libya is home to many tribes with different origins and circumstances, and no government will be able to satisfy all the demands of the various tribes. Therefore, even attempts to stabilize the regime will likely be met with tribal divisions and conflicts for the foreseeable future. It is a situation that calls for prayers to avoid further chaos and civil war.[32]

---

[32] According to a report by the United Nations Human Rights Council, Libya has an unstable political structure in which armed militias compete against each other for control, with the UN-recognized interim government, the Government of National Unity(GNU), governing the west and the warlord Libyan National Army(LNA) governing the east. In particular, crimes such as kidnapping and murder against immigrants and refugees are rampant, and the country is facing the worst human rights situation.(Mar. 27, 2023)
Mustafa Fetouri, "Libya's human rights situation is worse than what it was under Gaddafi", MIDDLE EAST MONITOR, 2023.04.13, https://www.middleeastmonitor.com/20230413-libyas-human-rights-situation-is-worse-than-what-it-was-under-gaddafi/

2) The paradox of the Arab democratic revolution, the synergetic effect of Western intervention plus the polarization of Middle Eastern dictatorships

There was an attempt to define these uprisings throughout the Middle East as a comprehensive 'democratization revolution.' From a Western perspective and consensus, the civil rebellion sparked by Tunisia could be a remarkable attempt at the democratization process against dictatorial authority throughout the Arab world. Even the process of disturbance and uprising was not focused on a political party or a counter-elite class. In the sense that the uprising was promoted in a voluntary form through a new communication structure, the so-called Social Network Service,[33] the West seems to be comparing it to the French Revolution, which the West defines

---

33 It is a general term for Internet-based community services that build connections and share information through online virtual spaces.

as the birth point of modern times.

But ironically, we can sense the deep-rooted distrust and sense of victimization in Arab society toward the West everywhere when we examine the cause and the results of the uprising in detail. As we know, the disturbance in Tunisia began with the Arabic youth who were driven out onto the streets by an economic dead end.[34] Internally, the incompetence of Arabic politics, especially the monarchy, military, and religious dictatorship, has led to corruption within Islam and brought hardship to the people. But Islam has shifted responsibility externally due to its religious pride and deep-rooted hostility toward the West, and it seems likely that it will continue to do so in the future. Also, it is undeniable that economic inequality between the West and the rest of the world is due to the economic structural side effects of Western hegemony and globalization executed by the West. Then, let's look at

---

34 Han Jin Um, 「Trigger of the Arab Spring」, 『The Arab Spring and Ten Years Thereafter』, snupress, 2022, p.4-6.

the countries such as Tunisia, Egypt, and Libya that have experienced national changes throughout turmoil in terms of the results. These countries may have taken advantage of the dictatorship internally, but at least they were the countries that left the door open to the West (even though they weren't pro-Western for some reason). Middle Eastern countries that established extreme dictatorships, such as Saudi Arabia and Iran, were able to manage disturbance in the Middle East under strict control even though internal turmoil and rebellion could have been expanded there.[35]

As a result, countries in the Middle East with closed, extreme religious, monarchy, and military dictatorships have deepened their hatred and vigilance toward the Western system. Rather than implanting the Western democratization model, there is a greater possibility that the connection to the

---

35 Gi Yeon Gu, 「Iran, unfinished revolution and civil disobedience movement」, 『The Arab Spring and Ten Years Thereafter』, snupress, 2022, p.208.

West itself will be considered as dangerous. This is because the West (through its Janus-like behavior of democratization and hegemony) has whenever shown the possibility of adding confusion by taking advantage of the internal disturbance in the Middle Eastern countries that have connections and exchanges.[36]

Chronological accumulation is a massive force that goes far beyond temporary timeliness. That's why observing the uprisings in the Middle East and figuring out the events only through temporal fragments can lead to the possibility of misjudgment. Historically, the conflict between the West and the Middle East has been tainted with hatred of the most profound and most significant magnitude than any other war or conflict. It is a severe prophecy testified by ancient biblical records that the conflict and hostility between Isaac and Ishmael of the Abrahamic lineage is a clash of spiritual roots between the

---

36 Amy Chua(2020), the book in front, p.107–110.

West and the Middle East.[37] Who would have thought that the document of ancient codes would become the main key code that dominates history of all times? It is practically the Cold War period (a century-long ideological conflict) that brought the greatest mental side effects on modern communities in the past century. However, it is a minor wound in terms of historical length and impact compared to the historical conflict between Isaac and Ishmael. For the Middle Easterns who imported Islam, the West was an unnegotiable hostile force for thousands of years. (Closely, the conflict between Israel and the Arabs, Western domination and oppression through World Wars I and II, the confrontation between Europe and the Turks, the Crusades, the confrontation between the Hellenic and Persian empires, etc.) Therefore, the intervention of the West is perceived as an unfortunate memory in most Middle Eastern countries. The reason why military dictators of Arab

---

[37] He will be a wild donkey of a man; his hand will be against everyone and everyone's hand against him, and he will live in hostility toward all his brothers.(Genesis 16:12)

monarchies and religions can continue to operate a closed system is not because the citizens give them absolute support. It can rather be seen as the result of a backlash following the intervention of Western powers.[38] In that sense, the idea that Western democratic systems are being implanted in Tunisia, Egypt, and Libya following the collapse of dictatorships is naive. Religious and political leaders who are operating a careless absolute-dictatorial system in the Middle East, such as Saudi Arabia and Iran, will once again confirm their hostility toward the West and educate their people explicitly. They will argue that (following the chaos surrounding Iraq, Libya, Egypt, etc.) Western powers' intervention and internal drive is a dangerous

---

[38] In 1951, Iranian Prime Minister Mohammad Mosaddegh, a nationalist leader, nationalized Iran's oil industry with the support of the Iranian people. In response, the British MI6 and the American CIA, whose interests were threatened, ousted Mosaddegh. It led to anti-foreign sentiment, which later joined forces with religious leaders to successfully carry out the Iranian Islamic Revolution in 1979, establishing a theocratic system with a supreme religious leader holding lifelong power.
Hyun Do Park(Sogang Euro-MENA Institute), 2023.
https://www.youtube.com/watch?v=2RI5Xa071mw

involvement and can cause great confusion and misfortune for their leadership and country. Furthermore, they also will justify internal regulation and isolation.

Middle East friendly toward the West and show thoughtless loyalty? The answer is not that simple. The elites will be aware of the economic damage to the Third World caused by the side effects of the globalization mechanism, and those who inherit Middle Eastern history intellectually and empirically are unlikely to be friendly toward the West. If the new system is stabilized, they will likely be uncomfortable with connections to the West. Of course, the West will seek someone who will represent their position and interests and request a friendly relationship by constant persuasion and collusion with the emerging powers of the Middle East. However, their counter-Middle East policy has consistently failed to earn absolute trust in that way.

3) Dictatorship and Islamic Extremism groups in Yemen, Egypt, and Libya

While dictatorship cannot be condoned in any way, considering the violent nature of Islamic extremism, it is undeniable that dictatorships in the Middle East, such as monarchies and military juntas, have inevitably suppressed the rise of Islamic extremism.

Islamic extremist groups, in that they justify their violence based on religious beliefs, makes their justification extremely radical. Gamal Abdel Nasser,[39] who came to power through a military coup and established a military dictatorship, initially showed interest in the extremist group, the Muslim Brotherhood, during his youth. He seized Egypt by exploiting their activities and cooperating with them, but soon later

---

[39] He actively pursued a foreign policy of neutralism and non-alignment by attending the Bandung Conference (Asian–African Conference). He resolved the Suez War, which broke out after the nationalization of the Suez Canal, with the support of international public opinion and then became a leader of Asia and Africa.

recognized the dangers of the Islamic extremist group and cracked down on them. Nasser's near assassination by the Muslim Brotherhood, the Islamic extremist group, made him realize that they were not a force that could be compromised under any political system. He responded with a ruthless crackdown, knowing that his life was in constant danger from their potential assassination attempts. President Sadat,[40] Nasser's political comrade and co-founder of the military regime, alternated between appeasement and oppression of the Muslim Brotherhood in an attempt to demonstrate his Islamic faith to the people. However, he was ultimately assassinated

---

[40] He believed that Egypt's reconstruction was impossible without peace with Israel. He successfully engaged the United States, which could exert pressure on Israel, to involve it in the Middle East peace process. Taking a pragmatic approach, he visited Israel in 1977 and paved the way for peace in the Middle East.

by them. Under the subsequent Mubarak[41] dictatorship, the Muslim Brotherhood faced intense repression and seemingly renounced their violence. However, with their emergence as the most potent political force in post-Mubarak Egypt, there is a need to be vigilant about the potential revival of their extremist violence should they come to power. Then, the only force in Egypt capable of preventing this regression will be the military.[42]

Muammar Gaddafi, the self-proclaimed "King of Kings" of Libya, used his dictatorship to control the country's fragmented

---

[41] Mubarak, a former Air Force commander, successfully stabilized the country by purging radical conservatives and weakening their power in the early days of his rule. However, in the process, he declared a state of emergency and implemented harsh measures that restricted civil liberties, which drew public backlash. Ultimately, he was forced to resign from the presidency on February 11, 2011, due to anti-government protests. In June 2012, he was sentenced to life imprisonment for the killing of protesters.

[42] Hyun Jung Ha, 「Egypt, A Return to the Old Issues of 'Bread, Freedom, Justice'」, 『The Arab Spring and Ten Years Thereafter』, snupress, 2022, p.42–44.

political landscape based on tribal divisions. He was extremely flexible in his dealings with the West, alternating between violent opposition and appeasement as long as it suited his interests. However, the one force he consistently opposed as a threat to his dictatorship and regime was neither the opposition tribes nor the West. It was the Islamic extremist group that he defined as irreconcilable enemies who sought to overthrow him, and his fears of them were hidden in his sensitive and nervous reactions.[43]

In Yemen, the central government is persistent in resisting popular protests. It is using every means at its disposal, including diplomatic maneuvering, authoritarian repression, and political appeasement, to maintain its precarious regime in the face of popular unrest. However, they are surprisingly apathetic about securing the southern region, a strategic stronghold

---

43 Han Baran and 7 others, 「Responses and implications of the Libyan situation by major countries」, 『Today's Global Economy』, Vol.11 No.27, Korea Institute for International Economic Policy, 2011.

of al-Qaeda,[44] taking advantage of the political turmoil. It is possible that they are too exhausted, wringing out their last bit of strength to prolong the life of the dictatorship. There is also the possibility that they are deliberately turning a blind eye to warn the West about the emergence of an extremist regime that could result from political turmoil. However, in conclusion, all of these attempts are extremely dangerous. Many countries in the Middle East are dominated by religious, political, and military dictatorships, which subject their people to harsh control and oppression. However, the unrest with no alternative is not simply a guarantee of democratization. The historical experience of the West and the Middle East is different, and the system of democratic governance through checks and balances that the West has built since the French Revolution is the result

---

[44] Islamic armed terrorist organization(anti-American, anti-Jewish) founded by Osama bin Laden from Saudi Arabia, who was identified as the force behind the 9/11 attacks in the United States. It was formed among Mujahideen who participated in the Soviet-Afghan war in the 1980s. Although weakened after bin Laden's death, the Iraqi branch merged with the Sunni militia and formed ISIS (Islamic State).

of a long history of systematic development.[45]

The overthrow of a dictatorship, without viable alternatives, often creates a favorable environment and foothold for Islamic extremists. The process of regimeization by Islamic extremists often involves a strategy of exploiting the chaos of the previous regime through their tacticians. The cases of Iran, Pakistan, and Sudan illustrate this. They induced political turmoil by taking advantage of the agitation of anti-regime elites and angry crowds to create chaos and then presented Islamic extremism as a legitimate governing ideology under the guise of 'revival.' It appealed to the masses and resisting elites, who were burdened by the historical sense of victimization from being exploited and distrusted by the West and also unwilling to return to the incompetence and oppression of the dictatorship. It was seen as an attractive alternative and governing model for them. Jihadists often lured Muslims by claiming that their suffering

---

45 Eui Hyun Hwang, 「Yemen, spring colder than winter」, 『The Arab Spring and Ten Years Thereafter』, snupress, 2022, p.85-98.

under dictatorship and Western rule was due to these systems not following the Quran, the word of Allah. They appealed to Muslims and made it sound irresistible by harkening back to the historical experience of the Prophet Muhammad's lifetime and promising a different kind of governance. However, naive Muslims often fail to grasp at first glance that this jihadist rhetoric is a fundamentally different proposition from what Islamic religious and political leaders mean when they speak of governance based on the Quran. While an Islamic system based on conscience and nationalism reinterpreted the Quran in terms of doctrine to subtly revise its violent history and function, the interpretation of the Quran by Islamic extremists accepted the Quran literally without understanding the historical context of the time when the Quran was revealed, thus moving toward justifying the use of violence.[46]

This is not a hypothetical model. Political rise, like the rise

---

[46] Encyclopedia Britannica Editors(2017), the book in front, p.236–241.

of the Islamic extremist forces in Iran, Pakistan, and Sudan, took place through the same process as described above. It is a reasonable assumption that Islamic extremist forces will exploit political turmoil in the future. It has been revealed through various sources that Osama bin Laden, in a statement shortly before his death, attempted to incite Islamic extremist forces and their regimes by exploiting the turmoil caused by the Middle East uprisings, in addition to his focus on fighting the West, including the United States.[47] This is surprising considering bin Laden's ideology. For him, the corruption of Islam was due to the intervention of Western powers, and the primary goal of his struggle was to eliminate the United States and Israel, the "head and root of all evil," before restoring the

---

[47] NBC Nightly News, "Bin Laden Documents Revealed | NBC Nightly News", NBC News, 2015.05.22, https://www.youtube.com/watch?v=qAJDqVudfPw

caliphate through the rule of Islamic extremism.[48] This suggests that bin Laden saw the Middle East uprisings as an opportune moment to strengthen Islamic extremism, even to the extent of reversing the order of his line of struggle.

There is a paradox of fear in Middle Eastern authoritarian regimes. While they often use fear-based politics to suppress dissent and maintain control, the dictators themselves paradoxically also have a deep fear of these opposition forces. Also, Islamic fundamentalism and tribal law, which are often the basis of these regimes, offer no mercy to those who have dishonored their family or clan.

Therefore, their thinking follows the authority of tribal families and is honored much more realistically than the state

---

[48] Bin Laden was primarily inspired by Sayyid Qutub's ideas, but insisted that Islamists should first focus on attacking the United States before targeting regional regimes or Israel as targets of overthrow. 9/11Commission, 「Final Report on Terrorist Attacks Upon the Unite States(The 9/11 Commission Report)」, 2004. p.54-55

system. In the Middle East, authoritarian power cannot exist without some degree of control over tribes and the legalistic system. Thus, even if some Middle Eastern authoritarian regimes were created through negotiations and compromises with certain tribes and the acceptance of Islamic law, the situation changes when the government is overthrown. The tribes that were previously hostile toward dictatorship and the Middle Eastern legalistic mindset of "an eye for an eye, a tooth for a tooth" lead to the extreme execution and revenge of dictators when they are pulled from power.[49] Mubarak of Egypt, Gaddafi of Libya, and Saleh of Yemen have either experienced this downfall or will follow a similar path. The once-absolute rulers of the Middle East are, in actuality, fearing the endless anger of the Islamic people being expressed in the form of Middle Eastern uprisings.

49　Amy Chua(2020), the book in front, p.101-110.

4) The collapse of the ruling system and Christianity

The old order in the Middle East is collapsing right now. Their own new order will also be sought. The turmoil in the Middle East, characterized by clashes between Islamic religious dictatorship, monarchical dictatorship, military dictatorship, Western modeling, and popular uprisings, is bound to create a desire for alternative models of a new order. Unfortunately, it seems highly unlikely that a new governance model will emerge under the sun in the Middle East. Some Christians in the Middle East may experience persecution as scapegoats of anger for the breakdown of order, which could further marginalize them. The clash with the inertia of the old order and persecution are always indispensable for the gospel to be testified. As a result, Christians could become ambiguous targets of persecution, potentially leading to extreme victimization such as social exclusion, displacement, or even refugees.[50] There have already been unprovoked attacks on Christians in Egypt and Syria. For a long time, Christians in the Middle East have not been active in evangelism in order to adapt to the Islamic system.

However, in many parts of the Middle East with long-standing antipathy against the West, there is little reluctance to describe the overthrow of a regime through popular uprising as democratization.[51] Democratization is a largely Western term and contextual interpretation. It is extremely rare for the entire Middle East to show such a positive and receptive attitude toward Western ideas. The old misconception that Christianity is equivalent to Western systems in Islamic societies is no longer true. Islam is externally a modified religious system that borrowed from Christianity in its early stages. They also tend

---

[50] Hyun Do Park, 「Arab Spring and Jihadi Salafis」, 『The Arab Spring and Ten Years Thereafter』, snupress, 2022, p.239-241.

[51] Han Jin Um, 「The meaning and status of democracy in Arab politics: a historical review.」, 『Democratization wave and local democracy』, Institute for Korean Democracy, 2012, p. 250-292.

to be more receptive to Christianity, which recognizes the one true God, than to Western rationalization, which excludes God altogether. The misunderstanding caused by the West's forceful approach to the Middle East (which longs for a new order) can be resolved through sacrifice and renunciation of the Gospel. It is an opportunity to talk about the true reign of Jesus through the gospel to refugees and others in the Middle East who were caused by the chaos through the unrest.

The unrest in the Middle East opens up the possibility of a new order being established in the Middle East, one that is not based on the earthly and hopeless system of Adam but on the gospel of heaven. Some Christians will only see it as dangerous, while others will approach it with faith that it is possible in the gospel.

Reference books and information

- Noam Chomsky·Gilbert Achcar, 「Perilous Power: The Middle East & U.S. Foreign Policy: Dialogues on Terror, Democracy, War, and Justice」, Routledge, 2006
- David Fromkin, 「A Peace to End All Peace: The Fall of the Ottoman Empire and the Creation of the Modern Middle East」, Holt Paperbacks, 2009
- Loretta Napoleoni, 「The Islamist Phoenix: The Islamic State(ISIS) and the Redrawing of the Middle East」, Seven Stories Press, 2014
- Ramzy Baroud, 「My Father was a Freedom Fighter: Gaza's Untold Story」, Pluto Press, 2010
- Dr. Richard Booker, 「Radical Islam's War Against Israel, Christianity, and the West」, Destiny Image Publishers, 2008
- Michael Weiss·Hassan Hassan, 「ISIS: Inside the Army of Terror」, Regan Arts, 2015
- Mark A. Gabriel, 「Islam And Terrorism」, Charisma House, 2002
- Compiled by Myongji Uni. Institute of Middle Eastern Affairs, 「Talk bout IS」, Mosinsaram, 2015
- Encyclopedia Britannica Editors, 「The Britannica Guide to the Islamic World」, Encyclopedia Britannica, Inc., 2009
- Samuel Laurent, Translated by Eun-Jung Felsner, 「IS Report」, Hanul Publishing Group, 2015
- Sayyid Qutb, 「Milesstone」, Islamic Book Service, 2006
- Ju Young Son, Byung Ha Hwang, etc. 「Walking the path of Islamic Civilization in 1400 years」, Prague, 2012
- Ira M. Lapidus, 「A History of Islamic Societies」, Cambridge University Press, 2002
- Alex Callinicos·Chris Harman & 3 others, 「Egyptian Revolution and popular revolt in Middle East」, Chaekgalpi, 2011
- Yamauchi Masayuki, Translated by Yong Bin Lee, 「The Tradegy of Islam」, Hanul Academy, 2017
- Amy Chua, 「Political Tribes: Group Instinct and the Fate of Nation」, Pengguin Books, 2019
- Yossef Bodansky, 「Bin Laden: The Man Who Declared War on America」, Prima Lifestyles, 2001
- William Wagner, 「How Islam Plans to Change the World」, Kregel Publications, 2004
- Tamara Sonn, 「Is Islam an Enemy of the West?(Global Futures)」, Polity, 2016
- Young Sik Ha, 「Conflict Reporter Young Sik Ha, talks about ISIS」, Bululabaramah, 2015
- Bernard Lewis, 「The World of Islam:Faith, People, Culture」, Thames & Hudson, 1980
- Ji Eun Lee(World Regional Research Center, Africa & Middle East Team, Professional Researcher), 「Changes in the situation in Israel and implications after Prime Minister Benjamin Netanyahu's return to power」, 「KIEP World Economic Focus」, Vol.6 No 6, Korea Institute for International Economic Policy, 2023
- 9/11Commission, 「Final Report on Terrorist Attacks Upon the Unite States (The 9/11 Commission Report)」, 2004

- Bains, P., Sugimoto, N., Wilson, C., 2022, 「BigTech in financial services: Regulatory approaches and architecture」, Fintech note 2022/002, IMF.
- Benedict R. O'G. Anderson, 「Imagined Communities: Reflections on the Origin and Spread of Nationalism」, 1983.
- Boissay, F., Ehlers, T., Gambacorta, L., Shin, H.S., 2021, 「Big techs in finance: on the new nexus between data privacy and competition」, BIS working papes No.970.
- Byung-Ock Chang, 「Articles : International Society ; The Conflict History of Chechnya-Russia - Focusing on Chechen's Islamist」, 「International Area Studies Review」, 13(1), The International Association of Area Studies, 2009, 513-530.
- Carstens, A., Claessens, S., Restoy, F., Shin, H.S., 2021, 「Regulating big techs in finance」, BIS Bulletin No.45.
- Crisanto, J.C., Ehrentraud, J., Lawson, A., Restoy, F., 2021, 「Big tech regulations: what is going on?」, FSI insights on policy implementation No.36, BIS.
- E. J. Hobsbawm, 「Nations and Nationalism since 1780」, Cambridge University Press, 2012.
- E J Hobsbawm, Terence O. Ranger, 「The Invention of Tradition」, Cambridge University Press, 1983.
- Gao Xiao, Continental Leader Xi Jinping, translated by Ha Jin Yi, Samho Media, 2012
- Gat Azar, Yacobson Alexander, 「Nations: The Long History and Deep Roots of Political Ethnicity and Nationalism」, Cambridge University Press, 2012.
- Geun-wook Lee, 「War in Afghanistan」, Hanul Academy, 2021.
- George Friedman, 「Flashpoints: The Emerging Crisis in Europe」, Anchor Books, 2016.
- Gérard Chaliand, Sophie Mousset, 「Question kurde à l'heure de Daech」, Hanul, 2018.
- Global Cooperation Headquarters, 「Digitally Looked Ukraine Russia Situation」, National Information Society Agency, 2022.
- Hanyang University Asia Pacific Research Center Russia and Eurasia Research Group, 「Conflicts in Post-Soviet Eurasia」, Minsokwon, 2014.
- Hanyang University Asia Pacific Research Center Russia Eurasia Research Group, 「Eurasia's national and ethnic identity」, Hanul Academy, 2010.
- Hans-Peter Martin, 「Game Over - Wohlstand fur wenige, Demokratie fur niemand, Nationalismus fur alle - und dann?」, Penguin Verlag Munchen, 2018.
- Hyun Seung -soo, Terrorism and conflict escalation in the Russian Federation's North Kavkaz, Conflicts in Post-Soviet Eurasia, Minsokwon, 2014
- KBS Documentary Insight Pandemic Money Production Team, 「Pandemic money」, Readers book, 2021.
- Margareta Mommsen, 「Das Putin-Syndikat (Russland im Griff der Geheimdienstler)」, C.H.Beck, 2017.
- Min Suk Kong, Structure of the U.S.-China Conflict: The hegemony competition after the financial crisis,

Reference books and information

threechairs, 2019.
- Niall Ferguson, 『Doom: The Politics of Catastrophe』, Penguin Press, 2021.
- Pascal Boniface, 『Geopolitics What is happening in the world right now?』, Guardian, 2019.
- Sang Ho, Son, 『Eight Challenges for Financial Innovation』, Korea Institute of Finance, 2022.
- Sejin Jung, 『Regional Studies: A Study on the Formation of the Identity of the Chechen People』, 『Journal of Russian
- Literature Research』, 44 Vol., Korean Association of Rusists, p.507-537, 2013.
- Sejin Jung, 『Russia Islam(History, ideology, war)』, Minsokwon, 2014.
- Sejin Jung, 『Происхождение Чеченской войны - через исторические конфликты между России и Чечни』, 『The Journal of Slavic Studies』, Vol.20 No.2, The Korean association of Slavic-Eurasian Studies, 2005, 355-386.
- Seong-jin Kim, 『Frozen Conflict in Moldova: Its Developments and Background』, 『Conflicts in Post-Soviet Eurasia』, Minsokwon, 2014.
- Shin, H.S., 2019, 『Big tech in finance: opportunities and risks』, BIS Annual Economic Report.
- Steven Lee Myers, 『The New Tsar: The Rise and Reign of Vladimir Putin』, Vintage Books USA, 2016.
- Sung Hoon Cho, 『Competition Policy for Big Techs and their Entry into Financial Services』, 『Capital Market Focus』, 2022-06, Korea Capital Market Institute.
- Wan Suk Hong, 『A Rough Road Ahead, Conflicts Between Russia and Chechenya : Causes, Developments and Prospect』, 『The Korean Political Science Association』, 39(5), 2005, 237-262.
- Walter Laqueur, 『Putinism: Russia and Its Future with the West』, Thomas Dunne Books, 2015.
- Yang Hyun Tak, 『Russian History: Principality of Kiev Rus Moscow, Russian Empire, Soviet Union, Russian Federation』, ePubple, 2020.
- Young Hoon Son, 『The development process of the Chechen-Russian War and national terrorism』, 『Conflicts in Post-Soviet Eurasia』, Misokwon, 2014, 117.
- Yong Sung Cho, 『The future 10 years of China』, Nexus BIZ, 2012.
- Limbach, Raymond. "Battle of Stalingrad". Encyclopedia Britannica, 15 Aug. 2021, https://www.britannica.com/event/Battle-of-Stalingrad. Accessed 6 April 2022.
- Historian Niall Ferguson Predicts the Future of China. https://youtu.be/IIApVciCScw 2022.2.27.
- Yuval Noah Harari, 『Why Vladimir Putin has already lost this war』, 『The Guardian Weekly』, 2022.03.28., https://www.theguardian.com/commentisfree/2022/feb/28/vladimir-putin-war-russia-ukraine
- https://www.bbc.com/ukrainian/news-60583913
- https://www.nytimes.com/2022/03/03/us/politics/russia-ukraine-military.html